The Scales of Justice

Trans-**action** Books

TA-1 Campus Power Struggle/ *Howard S. Becker*

TA-2 Cuban Communism/ *Irving Louis Horowitz*

TA-3 The Changing South/ *Raymond W. Mack*

TA-4 Where Medicine Fails/ *Anselm L. Strauss*

TA-5 The Sexual Scene/ *John H. Gagnon, William Simon*

TA-6 Black Experience:
Soul/ *Lee Rainwater*

TA-7 Black Experience:
The Transformation of Activism/ *August Meier*

TA-8 Law and Order:
Modern Criminals/ *James F. Short, Jr.*

TA-9 Law and Order:
The Scales of Justice/ *Abraham S. Blumberg*

TA-10 Social Science and National Policy/ *Fred R. Harris*

TA-11 Peace and the War Industry/ *Kenneth E. Boulding*

TA-12 America and the Asian Revolutions/ *Robert Jay Lifton*

The Scales of Justice

Edited by
ABRAHAM S. BLUMBERG

*Trans-***action** Books

Published and distributed by
Aldine Publishing Company

The essays in this book originally appeared
in *Trans-action* Magazine

Contents

Preface   vii

I. Introduction

Law and Order: The Counterfeit Crusade   1
Abraham S. Blumberg

II. In the Bargain Basement: The Sting of Justice

The Tipped Scales of American Justice   31
Stuart S. Nagel

Lawyers With Convictions   51
Abraham S. Blumberg

Winners and Losers: Garnishment and Bankruptcy   69
in Wisconsin
Herbert Jacob

III. The Lawyer as Champion

Lawyers for the Poor   91
Dallin H. Oaks / Warren Lehman

Advocacy in the Ghetto   105
Richard A. Cloward / Richard M. Elman

IV. Big Daddy Will Take Care of You

Justice Stumbles Over Science   123
David L. Bazelon

Juvenile Justice—Quest and Realities   141
Edwin M. Lemert

V. Pornography—Litmus Test of Liberty

Pornography—Raging Menace or Paper Tiger?   163
John H. Gagnon / William Simon

Selected Bibliography   177

Preface

However diverse their attitudes and interpretations may sometimes be, social scientists are now entering a period of shared realization that the United States—both at home and abroad—has entered a crucial period of transition. Indeed, the much burdened word "crisis" has now become a commonplace among black militants, Wall Street lawyers, housewives, and even professional politicians.

For the past six years, *Trans*-action magazine has dedicated itself to the task of reporting the strains and conflicts within the American system. But the magazine has done more than this. It has pioneered in social programs for changing the society, offered the kind of analysis that has permanently restructured the terms of the "dialogue" between peoples and publics, and offered the sort of prognosis that makes for real alterations in social and political policies directly affecting our lives.

The work done in the pages of *Trans*-action has crossed

disciplinary boundaries. This represents much more than simple cross-disciplinary "team efforts." It embodies rather a recognition that the social world cannot be easily carved into neat academic disciplines. That, indeed, the study of the experience of blacks in American ghettos, or the manifold uses and abuses of agencies of law enforcement, or the sorts of overseas policies that lead to the celebration of some dictatorships and the condemnation of others, can best be examined from many viewpoints and from the vantage points of many disciplines.

This series of books clearly demonstrates the superiority of starting with real world problems and searching out practical solutions, over the zealous guardianship of professional boundaries. Indeed, it is precisely this approach that has elicited enthusiastic support from leading American social scientists for this new and dynamic series of books.

The demands upon scholarship and scientific judgment are particularly stringent, for no one has been untouched by the current situation. Each essay republished in these volumes bears the imprint of the author's attempt to communicate his own experience of the crisis. Yet, despite the sense of urgency these papers exhibit, the editors feel that many have withstood the test of time, and match in durable interest the best of available social science literature. This collection of *Trans*-action articles, then, attempts to address itself to immediate issues without violating the basic insights derived from the classical literature in the various fields of social science.

The subject matter of these books concerns social changes that have aroused the long-standing needs and present-day anxieties of us all. These changes are in organizational life styles, concepts of human ability and intelligence, changing patterns of norms and morals, the relationship of social conditions to physical and biological environments, and in the status of social science with national policy making.

This has been a decade of dissident minorities, massive shifts in norms of social conduct, population explosions and urban expansions, and vast realignments between nations of the world. The social scientists involved as editors and authors of this *Trans*-action series have gone beyond observation of these critical areas, and have entered into the vital and difficult tasks of explanation and interpretation. They have defined issues in a way making solutions possible. They have provided answers as well as asked the right questions. Thus, this series should be conceived as the first collection dedicated not to the highlighting of social problems alone, but to establishing guidelines for social solutions based on the social sciences.

THE EDITORS
Trans-action

ℒaw and Order:
ℭhe ℭounterfeit ℭrusade

ABRAHAM S. BLUMBERG

No man is so exquisitely honest or upright in living, but brings all his actions and thoughts within compasse and danger of the lawes, and that ten times in his life might not lawfully be hanged.

Michael Montaigne
Of Vanitie, 1588

The task of the poet and the sociologist is ultimately the same: to search out and uncover the secret meaning of things. Yet, no combination of rhyme and meter or elaborate research methodology can capture the essence of the American mood as eloquently as the automobile bumper sticker. "When Guns Are Outlawed—Only Outlaws Will Have Guns," "Support Your Local Police," "I Fight Poverty —I Work," "Remember The Pueblo," "Bury Communism," "America: Love It or Leave It," "New York State—Land of High Taxes," are exclamations of the anger, thwarted

1

hopes, and righteous indignation of an ordinarily taciturn middle mass of Americans, for whom the American Dream has turned to ashes. Mountains of heavily mortgaged goods have not brought them the comfort, security and joy promised by the mass media, if only they would consume. On the contrary, the typical American, *white or black,* expresses intensified anxiety about and preoccupation with crime and lawlessness, according to a recent Gallup Poll study. The survey revealed that 75 percent of those polled felt that the law courts in the United States are "too soft" toward criminals. "Crime and lawlessness" topped the list when people were asked about problems facing their communities, ahead of such local problems as crowded schools, transportation, and high taxes. Small wonder then, that the "law and order" theme has such incredible appeal, supplanting the theme of "Communism" in political campaigns at the national and local level.

The relationship of the current themes of "law and order" and "crime in the streets" to the growing resentments and belligerence of the middle mass will tend to dominate the politics and social life of America in the decade ahead. As the struggle unfolds there will undoubtedly be shifts in alliances, new targets, new slogans to match new grievances, and new violence and disorder. What is certain is that the legal system, the enforcement apparatus and the courts as political instruments, will be at the center of the social upheavals that are bound to occur. Rather than the traditionally passive role ascribed to them by Marx and Mills, the middle mass is going to perform a critical function in determining the directions we are likely to travel in shaping our legal institutions, in either preserving or destroying the remnants of democracy in America.

The usual sociological categories of lower middle-class,

blue-collar or white-collar, working class, salariat, and lumpenbourgeoisie are meaningless and often inadequate in helping us assess the sources of their anguish and distress. Who are the members of the middle mass? The sociological stereotype of the middle-mass man is characterized by a series of rather well defined social-psychological traits. Possessed of simplistic views of the world, he tends to see the society he lives in through the lens of very limited experience, meager education, and in terms of his knowledge of people very much like himself. His simplistic views are the source of his intolerance for anything "un-American." Having very little real knowledge or experience of contrasting life styles, he is likely to mistrust the new, the strange, the different, the intellectual, the "arty." He reveres authority, masculinity, physical prowess, and is profoundly patriotic. His tolerance, if any, for sexual misconduct, the atheist, the homosexual, extreme styles in clothing or hair, or deviant behavior of any kind is rather low. He tends to dichotomize between we-they, friends-strangers. In a world organized along impersonal, bureaucratic lines he feels powerless, not only because of his earlier deprivations and insecurity, but because his sense of marginality is intensified by a lack of academic and technical credentials. He sees the world as a Hobbesian jungle where only the powerful, the lucky, or those with "pull" and connections prevail. Because he feels he has so little bargaining power, he tends to be pessimistic about his future as insulation against disappointment and failure.

The conventional sociological conceptions of the working-class life-style are not wholly adequate in explaining why it is that the working class—read middle mass—has become the backbone of support for that call to arms, "Law and Order." More to the point is the fact that as an economic group they are to be found somewhere between the welfare poor and the educated professional and white-collar technicians. They earn anywhere from $5,000 to $10,000 per year in a nation where the median income before taxes for a family in 1967 was reported by the U. S. Department of Commerce as $8,000 per year. Since a $9,000 per year is said to be a modest but adequate income, many of the middle-mass families are therefore in great difficulty. The myth of American affluence is punctured by the fact that the middle mass consists of almost 80,000,000 persons in some 23,000,000 families who are waist deep in debt, and almost half of the breadwinners of the group have never gone beyond the eighth grade. Many depend on more than one income and/or "moonlighting" to maintain precarious, marginal incomes which are also being depleted by inflation. For many of them the mindless fare of television, the synthetic excitements of gambling, the race track, pro football, and the circus escapism of the space program, serve to relieve the endless tedium of a life that at best is a series of traps.

It would be easy to dismiss the law and order slogan as a code phrase for repression of an increasingly black urban proletariat by a predominantly white, flag-waving, lower middle-class group of troglodytes. Yet such a simplistic racial explanation only serves to conceal the subtleties of class conflict that have been part of the American landscape since Shays' Rebellion. This was an armed insurrection by debtor farmers against the merchants, politicians, and lawyers of the Massachusetts seaboard towns who were using the legislature and courts to levy high taxes, foreclose mortgages and imprison debtors. Another variation of class conflict and violence in American history is that of a recurring phenomenon of an "in-between" class which is oppressed and exploited by a more privileged group from above and threatened by an emerging group from below.

Examples of this situation may be observed in the Whiskey Rebellion of 1791-1794, when the Scots-Irish of Pennsylvania were in-between the Indians and the wealthy Quakers; the Know-Nothing riots, where an urban, Protestant proletariat was in-between newly arrived Catholics and rich industrialists; and the Draft Riots of 1863, which found the Irish Catholic workers in-between blacks who had recently won their freedom, and a Protestant aristocracy.

As in the past, nothing has been done to reduce the tension and sources of conflict that exist as a consequence of increasing pressure of the poor black, Puerto Rican, Mexican underclass or the in-between middle mass. On the contrary, at virtually every economic, social and political friction-point, the existing conflicts have been exacerbated. In the significant areas of voting rights, education, skilled jobs, unions, and housing, law and order is invariably invoked to delay, obstruct, deflect or vitiate—to keep the "outs" out and the "ins" in. In this context law and order is a we-they dichotomy, a double standard for sanctifying existing social and legal arrangements. An even more cynical aspect of the situation is the extent to which America's upper and upper-middle classes require the middle mass to bear a good deal of the economic and social freight in their meager subsidy of the bottom poor (20 percent of the population with but 5 percent of its income). Invariably, whether the issues in conflict are jobs, housing, or schools, it is the middle mass and the poor who are locked in struggle, while the social strata above them are nesting safely away from the fray in protected businesses or professions, genteel suburbs and private schools.

At the economic level the middle mass pays much more than its share of income taxes. Tax avoidance loopholes simply mean that the middle mass must pay taxes not paid by an H. L. Hunt or a J. Paul Getty. The great bulk of social security taxes are paid by the middle mass since the tax is levied on almost everything they earn. Public education, hospitals and welfare are largely funded through their local property taxes, sales taxes and excise taxes. Although the middle mass largely funds the lavish space program as well as the much more limited poverty program, they resent only the latter. Their attitude is best summed up in the unlikely acronym of a racist group called Sponge—Society for the Prevention of Negroes Getting Everything.

Middle-mass housing is rapidly deteriorating, its refuse collection is erratic, its parks in shambles, its water and sewer facilities of dubious quality. Nevertheless, the middle-mass man seldom establishes any sort of connection between his shoddy existence and the fact that during the fiscal year of 1968, for example, the federal government spent sixty-three cents of every tax dollar for the military, space and Vietnam, and only two cents for housing and community development. Instead, he attributes the deteriorating quality of his life, his helplessness, his disappointments and frustrations to a breakdown in law and order, the "nigger," "spic," Indian, or whatever group is threatening to him. He perceives existing poverty programs as a free handout to those who will not work, and from which he derives no benefit. His sense of alienation and mistrust of government has led to the stockpiling of handguns and rifles, and a growing vigilantism.

Law and order has become an ideology which serves to distort and disrupt relations between the middle mass and the bottom, separating them into hostile enclaves which are in continuous confrontation. Although there are many areas of their lives which are of common interest and concern (housing, health, transportation, education, employment, environmental problems, etc.) and about which their objectives are quite similar, they are polarized by the ideology of law and order. But there is an even more basic problem. Central to the notion of law and order is the promise that it will provide the machinery for orderly change in the allocation of rewards, opportunity structures, and access to the means of life in our social system; in a word, justice. Therefore, it is said, there is no need to resort to guns or bayonets to redress grievances or to effect social change. The ballot box, the legislature, the court, the administrative tribunal, will right wrongs before irremediable harm is inflicted and inequities reach explosive proportions.

What is at once vexing and embarrassing about the pledges that are embodied in the law and order concept is that they are almost at once unredeemed, if not denied outright, by our society's institutional arrangements for carrying them out. Our law enforcement, public welfare, and court systems have become the very agencies which blunt the possibilities of orderly change, and the more equitable allocation of life chances. Creditors, landlords, corporations, the wealthy, and the political machines, tend to receive more favorable treatment by the courts, legislatures and regulatory agencies because of particularism, private contractual agreements, and favorable political arrangements which have the sanction of long usage. On the other hand, consumers, debtors, wage-earners, the very young, the mentally ill, the deviant and poor tend to receive rather less favorable treatment from courts, legislatures and regulatory agencies. The former groups tend to receive the *substance,* the latter groups, the *form* of justice. This aspect of the ideological nature of the law and order slogan can best be examined within the context of the handling of the criminal, the debtor, the delinquent, and the mentally ill in our legal system.

We owe an everlasting intellectual debt to Emile Durkheim for his insightful notion that crime is an inevitable feature of social structure—"crime is normal because a society exempt from it is utterly impossible." Durkheim's classic formulation provides us with a timeless sense of perspective in contemplating the meaning and pervasiveness of crime and deviance in the human situation, a perspective that transcends the recurring hysteria epitomized in the current catch-all political slogans. Criminologists with an interest in history recognize that ours is not the best nor the worst of times in producing criminals, riots, assorted villains, social deviants, grim deeds of violence, genocide, murder, and vigilantism. While the technology for inflicting harm upon others has become both more available and more dangerous, it is probably safer to walk the streets of an American city today than those of medieval Italy or even Manhattan of fifty years ago. It is abundantly clear that Durkheim's analysis is confirmed by compelling historical evidence, and it should therefore not surprise us that most (if not all) of us, have violated legal norms on more than one occasion without being labelled delinquent or criminal.

No matter which version of the official crime statistics one accepts, it is quite evident that very few of us are brought to book, i.e. apprehended, processed in the official enforcement and court machinery, and adjudicated as criminals and delinquents. Any society that committed the energy, resources and personnel to root out and punish all wrongdoers would set off enough mass paranoia, violent conflict and savage repression to become a charnel house, and pass into oblivion. On the other hand, every society tends to produce its quotient of crime and deviance and an accompanying apparatus to sort out those malefactors deemed most suitable for processing—usually those persons and kind of behavior readily vulnerable.

Modern crime may be said to exist at four broadly distinct levels of occurrence. The most profitable and involving the least amount of risk is *Upperworld* crime—it is the least susceptible to the official enforcement machinery, and is only rarely represented in the Uniform Crime Reports of the F. B. I. Upperworld crime is carefully planned like a military campaign in the walnut-panelled executive suites of corporations with billions of dollars in assets, in state houses, in country clubs. Quite often the criminal venture is simply thought of by the participants as shrewd business strategy calculated to produce a profit or to perform a "service" for the consumer, the voter, or some other constituency, often at the latter's expense. "The Great Electrical Conspiracy" involving General Electric and Westinghouse, among others, the speculations of Billie Sol Estes and the activities of the corporate and federal officials without whose help he could not have succeeded, the activities of Bobby Baker, the frauds and larceny connected with the federal highway program, and the drug scandals are but a few of the more recent illustrations of the exorbitantly profitable criminal activities that take place at the upperworld level. The *Wall Street Journal* and *Consumer Reports* are often better records of criminal activities at this level than the official enforcement agencies such as the Food and Drug Commission or the Anti-Trust Division. The latter agencies are quite ineffectual in dealing with the social harm ultimately inflicted by upperworld activities; prosecution of violators at this level is a relatively unusual occurrence.

Related to upperworld crime, especially at the level of the political machine, is *Organized* crime. The local political machines that ordinarily control local police and court officials afford the protection organized crime requires for its functioning. Its activities cut across state lines and national boundaries and range from legitimate enterprises such as labor unions to activities which cater to appetites and pursuits forbidden by penal codes—gambling, usury, drugs, pornography and prostitution. Very little beyond the conjectural is known about organized crime and organized criminals except that they are seldom grist for the mill of the conventional police, prosecution and court process. At the moment, the F.B.I. and local enforcement agencies probably have more resources and undercover agents operating in student organizations, black organizations, on campuses and in pursuit of drug users than they have invested in studying the area of organized crime.

The third level of crime, *Political* crime, is one that we do not overtly recognize, except possibly in connection with our treason or sedition laws. Eugene V. Debs and Alger Hiss are our most notable political criminals, and most recently Dr. Benjamin Spock was almost added to the list. In many instances the political criminal is not actually convicted for the substance of the real grievance we harbor against him, but for a legalistic substitute; in the case of Alger Hiss, it was for perjury.

The fourth and least honorific level of crime is often the least remunerative, least protected, and of the sort most readily available to lower-strata persons of the middle mass and bottom poor because of their limited range of skills and circumscribed options of action, and may be called *Commonplace* crime. Except for some confidence men and other professional-career criminals whose activities may bring them into the world of organized and upperworld crime, crime at this level ranges from shoplifting to armed robbery. It is usually the most visible sort of criminal activity and therefore the most vulnerable to the official instruments of law enforcement. For example, one-third of all arrests in America are for some variation of the prosaic charge of drunkenness or public intoxication, the usual variations being "intoxicated driver," "drunk in a public place," "drunk and disorderly," or an old favorite, "drunk and resisting arrest." Violators at this level of criminal activity constitute the great bulk of crimes which are duly reported in the Uniform Crime Reports of the F.B.I. in any given year.

The history of those crimes that tend to jam our courts is quite clear. Moral entrepreneurs are outraged by behavior they perceive as odious and thereupon invoke the righteous indignation of legislators who enact penal statutes calculated to inhibit, deter and, or punish the behavior complained of (fornication, vagrancy, gambling, disorderly conduct, sodomy, lewdness, lascivious carriage, drunkenness, prostitution, possession of marijuana, abortion, homosexuality, etc.). Penal codes are attempting to regulate areas of human conduct that would require, for their proper enforcement, the installation of a telescreen in every bedroom. The sweep of the criminal sanction has become so great that administrative enforcement of some of our laws —for example our vehicle and traffic laws—has become a joke. How many of the fifty thousand automobile deaths each year are really homicides, not accidents? Each year there are over four million auto injuries. How many of these are in reality attempted homicides, or felonious assaults with the automobile as the weapon? How many of these deaths and injuries are the consequence of culpable negligence, shoddy workmanship and greed, which are incident to a production process calculated to stimulate consumption rather than a concern for the consumer? Consumer frauds involving shady credit practices as well as outright larceny, account for an annual take far in excess of all robberies and burglaries combined. In 1967, the F.B.I. reported that property valued at $1.4 billion was stolen as a result of all robberies, burglaries, larcenies, and auto thefts commited that year. By way of contrast the amount stolen annually, in the field of home improvement alone, is in excess of one billion dollars. The gross revenue from loan-sharking, which is but a single activity of organized crime, is thought to produce profits in the multi-billion dollar range. The take from illegal gambling is said to be $20 billion each year.

Nevertheless, a good deal of administrative time and resources of our criminal process are devoted to areas that are not appropriately suited to the criminal process, and instead simply clog the channels of enforcement, relegating more serious conduct to a secondary priority. Surely the removal of abortion, vagrancy, drunkenness, disorderly conduct, prostitution, drug usage, most so-called sex offenses, as the stuff of the criminal process, would not only free the system for more urgent crime control, but would help speed the development of more humane alternatives to many of the problems we have conveniently shunted into the criminal arena—mainly because it appears to be cheap and makes us feel so morally righteous and secure.

In summary, our penal sanctions, our law enforcement and court bureaucracies that administer them, are in large measure organized and geared to detecting, sorting out and adjudicating the kinds of crimes and delinquencies most often and most visibly engaged in by the socially marginal strata. The selection of suitable candidates for the adjudication process (crime, delinquency, or mental illness) is not some version of a roulette game, but has fairly well defined limits, which have been imposed by the stratification system. The clients served by our enforcement, criminal court, public mental hospital, prison, parole and other "rehabilitation" systems are overwhelmingly drawn from segments of the middle mass and bottom poor.

The harsh fact is that our criminal process, especially

at the initial stages of enforcement, is primarily oriented to bureaucratic goals of efficiency and production rather than any humanistic goals of the rule of law. Those persons and modes of conduct that are most visible and most opprobrious in that they offend the values of dominant social groups, become suitable subjects for labelling as deviants and criminals by the very nature of our lavish criminal sanctions. As a consequence, the annual edition of the Uniform Crime Reports of the F.B.I. consistently indicates that the very young, the black, urban, poor and largely male group constitutes the American crime problem. We know this to be an absurdity, but we go on appropriating vast sums in support of an enforcement apparatus that produces the same result for our money year after year.

The enforcement and adjudication process boils down to this: Intolerably large caseloads of defendants in our criminal justice system, which must be disposed of in an organizational context of limited resources, encourages police, prosecution, and court personnel to be concerned largely with strategies that lead to a guilty plea. In this connection rather frank and revealing statements about the criminal courts were made by a federal judge and a New York City judge and appeared recently in *The New York Times:*

> The life of a Criminal Court judge has been described as "generally degrading" and the system of justice has been condemned as "dehumanizing" by one of the city's newest judges, former License Commissioner Joel L. Tyler. . . . "You sit on that bench," Judge Tyler said, "and you get this terrible sense that you can't help anyone who could be helped. Sometimes you look at a young man or woman and you feel that if someone could really get hold of them maybe something good could come of their lives . . . But the

system is just too big, the individual is nothing, the lawyers are ciphers and the judge turns out to be a virtual mechanic more often than not."

In the course of a two hour interview, Judge Tyler criticized the handling of narcotics addicts ("It's fantastic, crazy—we march them into the sea like lemmings"); the lawyers for the Legal Aid Society, who handle most arraignments ("They don't fight hard enough"); and the facilities of some of the parts of the Criminal Court ("The traffic courts are a disgrace; the Brooklyn Criminal Court is a rat hole").

But Judge Tyler said that the frustrations of his job went far deeper than the lack of proper physical facilities.

"First," he said, "you get so many cases stacked up you don't have time to really consider the individual . . . At arraignment you may have a minute with each person. Most of them are narcotics addicts, and if you let them go, you know they will be right back on the stuff. If you hold them on bail—most don't make it— they are thrown eventually into a program that is of doubtful value."

The judge was referring to the city's narcotic rehabilitation program, which is based mainly on confronting addicts with their problems through group therapy. It is the leading program in use at Rikers Island prison.

"I think it is crazy, plain stupid, to treat addicts as criminals," he said. "And the theory on which the rehabilitation program is based, that addiction is curable, well, I'd like to see their experience, their statistics. I believe it's damn low, their rate of cure."

Does he have any hope for the administration of criminal justice here? "Not much, but enough to kick about it," he said. "The older judges, some of them, tell me that they started like I did, mad as hell, wanting to reform things, but finally they realized you can't beat the system. When I get to that point I'll hand in my papers."

In a similar vein, J. Skelly Wright, a noted federal judge writes:

Despite the presumption of innocence, the defendant in these police and magistrate courts is, prima facie, guilty. The burden is placed upon him to give a satisfactory answer to the question, "What have you got to say for yourself?" He is almost always uncounselled and sometimes he is not even informed of the charges against him until after the so-called trial. Often no records are kept of the proceedings, and in the overwhelming majority of cases these courts are, in practice, courts of last resort. The careful provisions for appeal, certiorari and habeas corpus, which look so fair in the statute books, are almost a dead letter as far as indigent misdemeanor defendants are concerned.

The police and their supporters in the legislatures and the mass media have perpetuated the myth that the U. S. Supreme Court through its rulings has promoted a crime wave. But a close examination of our history reveals that we have always been in the midst of a "crime wave." For example, the Mapp decision excluding illegally obtained evidence did not come until 1961, after a long history of abuses at the local level by police authorities who searched people, their homes, and personal effects almost at will, and generally maltreated them in the process. The requirement that indigent defendants in felony cases be provided with counsel did not come until 1963 in the Gideon case. The Miranda ruling in 1966 aroused the special fury of police buffs and supporters of the law and order ideology. All Miranda did was to extend to the poor, the naive, the ignorant, the uneducated, the insecure and frightened person who found himself in the coercive atmosphere of police interrogation, the privilege against self-incrimination that had always been secured for the educated, the socially privileged, the counseled, the knowledgeable, and the professional criminal. All Miranda did was require that *every* person arrested be advised that what he said may be used against him, that he had a right to remain silent, and a right to a lawyer. What was good enough for the professional and organized criminal was certainly good enough for the ordinary person. Miranda and the other decisions simply spelled out rights declared in our Constitution over one hundred and fifty years ago. It is well to remember that prior to these decisions it was not uncommon for police and enforcement officials to kick doors down, to search in a fishing-expedition fashion, to apply the rubber hose to one's back or genitals, or to aim a well placed blow to the side of the head with a phone book, in order to encourage people to "confess." Indeed, the Supreme Court sought to establish a sense of order and decency in an area which had become a quagmire of police lawlessness in the various states. It is perhaps noteworthy that the British have operated under the Judges Rules for over fifty years, guaranteeing the sort of rights covered by Miranda. Germany, France and Sweden have similar rules, without the sort of querulous foot-dragging our own police have manifested.

The irony of the attacks on the Supreme Court over Miranda is that research returns indicate that it has not hampered the police at all. It is estimated that only about 20 percent of *all* crime is ever reported and that only approximately 25 percent of this total is cleared by an arrest being made. But confessions have never been an important element in this rather low overall clearance rate, which has generally depended on independent evidence and the testimony of witnesses. In spite of Miranda, people continue to confess even after warnings have been given, and the endless crush of cases in our courts and the overcrowding of our prisons continue. In some communities the police have virtually ignored Miranda. Some lawyers and judges had hoped that one of the by-products of the court's rulings would be an overhauling of the American police system, an upgrading of the personnel and administrative procedures affecting the almost 500,000 police and the over 40,000 departments. To a very limited extent there have been some reforms of major abuses, but not without some ominous developments of police politicization which are potentially destructive of the democratic process.

The law and order mystique of America possesses a rather fascinating internal inconsistency. At the international level, for example, although the United States promoted the 1925 Geneva treaty prohibiting the use of gas and germ warfare, we have never ratified it, although the major "outlaw" communist nations have done so. At the national level, the law and order ideology conveniently ignores the kind of lawlessness inherent in the failure to implement the 1954 Supreme Court decision of Brown vs. the Board of Education, and the fudging on school-guidelines. The most vehement law and order adherents heap calumny on the Supreme Court, but also oppose gun-control legislation as a step toward crime prevention. Their counterparts in the various enforcement bureaucracies in their cruel harassment of drug-users and physicians have deliberately chosen to ignore   legal doctrine established in Lindner vs. United States, 268 U. S. 5 (1925) which would treat addiction as a disease, and the addict as a sick person for whom the medical profession could legally prescribe and treat in the course of private practice. In spite of the enactment of ever more punitive measures in dealing with addiction, the number of addicts grows, setting off a further chain reaction of criminality by those who cannot get the needed drugs except through illicit means. It is an obsession of the law and order ideologist that the "junkie" is a criminal, conveniently ignoring that it is their own lawless sangfroid that has achieved the very criminal results they seemingly seek to avoid. The law and order crusade has also encouraged the use of draft laws to intimidate, silence, restrain or even imprison our young people, rather than for the basic purposes of defense for which those laws were originally drawn. Illicit wiretapping and bugging are endemic, the F.B.I. has been employed on more than one occasion as a not-too-subtle vehicle to stifle criticism, as in the case of the "investigation" of individuals who gave testimony about hunger in America.

Although our bail laws are in effect an insidious form of preventive detention, there are well-organized efforts at the federal and local level to formalize these procedures, which are ostensibly designed only for dangerous offenders who are likely to commit crimes while on bail or parole. The crucial feature of the preventive-detention proposals is, how does one predict who will commit a crime that threatens life and limb? Once we go down this road, we might as well start building the concentration camps at once, because our local short-term detention jails are too crowded, and we would need much more room as we make our predictions about individual cases. Of course we have ample precedents for this practice. In 1942 we removed and "relocated" to internment camps 112,000 persons of Japanese ancestry, although not a single one of them was ever found guilty of any act of sabotage or espionage. One of the most common forms of preventive detention occurs in the case of the over 500,000 mentally ill persons who are at any given time detained in prison-like mental hospitals without ever having been convicted of a crime; they are held on the basis of psychiatric predictions about their *possible* behavior.

The role of the middle mass in influencing the direction of the law and order crusade is best demonstrated by the "stop and frisk" decision of the Supreme Court. State legislatures taking cognizance of the fact that police were not observing the standard of probable cause (a reasonable belief that a crime has been committed and that the accused is the perpetrator) as a basis for search and arrest, passed stop and frisk legislation. Stop and frisk wrote into law a much lower standard of reasonable suspicion as grounds for the police to stop and interrogate persons in the street and frisk them for a possible weapon. Thus, police were given statutory and, in some instances, judicial comfort and support for that which they were doing anyway when they were fabricating "probable cause." It is noteworthy, however, that the President's Commission on Law Enforcement and Administration of Justice (popularly known as the Crime Commission) indicated in its report that stop and frisk power has generally been employed by the police against the inhabitants of our urban slums, against racial minorities and the underprivileged. Police will make "field interrogations" of people, simply because their clothing, hair, gait or other mannerisms square with preconceived police notions of who is suspicious—quite often these are Negroes, Puerto Ricans, Mexicans, Indians. Police practice of illegal arrests on suspicion or for investigation rather than probable cause were fairly widespread prior to the passage of stop and frisk legislation, especially in neighborhoods inhabited by the poor and racial minorities. Many of these arrests (about 300,000 per year) are made as part of an "aggressive patrol" tactic to demonstrate police muscle, as well as a fishing expedition. Most of these arrests are terminated without any formal charge being brought.

In June, 1968, the United States Supreme Court—anticipating an election in which Nixon, Humphrey and Wallace ran as law and order candidates, and sensitive to the middle-mass concern with crime—upheld the stop and frisk practices of the police. With this decision, we can mark the turning point in the increasing pressure that the law and order ideologues will yet bring to neutralize the Bill of Rights.

The stop and frisk practices of the police were sanctioned on the ground that the intrusion upon the person occasioned by the "stop" was justified if a policeman reasonably suspected a crime was afoot, or if he felt there was a danger to himself or others. The lone dissent of Justice Douglas is of interest. "To give the police greater power than a magistrate is to take a long step down the totalitarian path . . . if the individual is no longer to be sovereign, if the police can pick him up whenever they do not like the cut of his jib, if they can 'seize' and 'search' him in their discretion, we enter a new regime."

A police manual's instructions as to the methods to be employed for a frisk are worth recording. Keep in mind that the subject of the search, which takes place usually in public, is standing facing a wall with his hands raised. *"The officer must feel with sensitive fingers every portion of the prisoner's body. A thorough search must be made of the prisoner's arms and armpits, waistline and back, the groin and area about the testicles, the entire surface of the legs down to the feet."* This is no "petty indignity" or "minor intrusion," and it may now be employed by any policeman who feels a "reasonable" suspicion—and of course a policeman may always feel that he is in danger. Police now have virtually unlimited power over our lives, for the Supreme Court will not be there to supervise the propriety of the stops and frisks that may take place only because they are a useful harassment device.

Despite the rather elaborate instruments of control now available to the law and order crusade—an 80 to 90 percent conviction rate, electronic eavesdropping and other more elaborate technologies, stop and frisk, a bail system that amounts to preventive detention, and overflowing prisons and mental hospitals—the middle mass remains sold on the notion that more of the same is the answer to the crime problem. They have bought the illusion of a crime-free society and are almost ready to accept some version of a blue-coated garrison state to achieve it. In pursuit of order, we will create a more sophisticated crime-control technology and more elaborate controls over the lives of all of us. The middle mass is deceived by the law and order ideology in that it promises that one can achieve "peace of mind" and the "good life" without addressing ourselves to the underlying issues of poverty, race, housing, education, health, and employment.

In still another way has the law and order ideology served to conceal one of the real problems of the middle mass. The middle mass has not saved any of its righteous indignation for the shameless manner in which our civil courts act as collection agencies for the merchants and finance companies that all too often beguile them into buying goods they cannot afford at prices bloated by interest, service, and insurance charges.

As of 1967, our national consumer debt amounted to almost $100 billion. Most people are in debt in some fashion. The average annual rates of interest charged on many of the loans involving installment contracts range from 18 to 42 percent. In virtually every state in the union these are "seller's contracts" in that they are lawfully designed to give every possible legal advantage to the seller in advance of the sale, with very limited recourse by the buyer should the goods be defective, and the performance or services incomplete. There are four major weapons that are written into the various state laws that are used by the seller against the buyer: first, a "confession of judgment" in which the purchaser signs away any rights to a court defense in advance; second, garnishment laws, which permit the seller to exact a portion of the purchaser's wages, should he miss an installment (in California a creditor can garnish up to 50 percent of a buyer's wages); third, repossession laws which permit the seller to exact continued payments, even after the article has been repossessed from the purchaser because of nonpayment; fourth, "add on" provisions in installment contracts, which make previous purchases, even though they have been paid for, serve as security for new purchases. Thus, in the latter instance, a person may have liquidated a $1,000 debt for furniture, but have it seized and sold to satisfy a new debt for a TV set, for which he has missed payments! Wage assignments are another device employed by sellers to trap the unwary. When such an agreement is signed an employer is authorized to turn over a share of the debtor's wages to his creditor without a court judgment, should there be a default in the payments. Many consumers are virtually trapped into these unconscionable agreements which consign them to garnishment, loss of job and public dependency because of the insensitivity of our legislatures and civil courts to their plight. Only three states—Texas, Pennsylvania and Florida—have banned garnishment. The notorious device of "sewer service," which results in a debtor defendant never being notified of an action pending against him, results in a 95 percent rate of default judgments in New York City, because the debtor has not appeared to defend himself. The doctrine protecting the "holder in due course" of consumer commercial paper serves as a cover for many consumer frauds. In some instances the seller and the finance company are in reality one and the same party, with the installment contract being "sold" to a finance company to take advantage of the fact that the usual defenses of fraud or defect in the article cannot be raised in many instances against a "holder in due course."

Our legal system has an amazing degree of confidence in the capacity of lawyers and psychiatrists to hold the machinery of the system together. There is an almost innocent faith in the ability of these caretakers to make the criminal courts, civil courts, juvenile courts and mental hospitals function. The Supreme Court decisions in Miranda and Gault, for example, depend greatly on the lawyer to bring them to the level of working reality. In the case of Gault, it will be recalled, virtually all of the procedural safeguards of the adult court were made to apply to juvenile court. Questions as to whether the proceeding is civil or criminal, and such matters as the right to appeal and the evidentiary standards to be applied, all remain in doubt. In any event, there has been an agonizing reappraisal of the very agency that had as its historic mission the saving of children. But the real problem of the juvenile court is not just a legalistic one (although it really was a dishonest ploy to claim all these years that the protection of children did not require the constitutional safeguards afforded adult criminals). It is that, in the words of Albert K. Cohen, "Like Christianity the juvenile court philosophy has never really been tried." Certainly *every* child should have *every* constitutional safeguard that we apply to adults

—and then some. Just to furnish him with a lawyer and the other safeguards is not the heart of the matter. The root of the problem is resources—money. With the increasing precariousness of the nuclear family, virtually every problem in connection with child socialization has been dumped into other institutional frameworks, especially the school. When they fail, the juvenile court becomes the "trash bin" of all the unsolved problems. Additional legal services are not the key issue at all. If anything, two recent studies appear to indicate that something uncomfortably close to cooptation of juvenile court lawyers occurs anyhow, so we're right back to the real issue—more resources to care for troubled children and, one hopes, less punitive juvenile courts.

There is one aspect of the juvenile court that needs to be emphasized and researched more carefully: the real scene of all the action is "intake," not the formal court proceeding itself. That is where all the bargains are struck and the real decisions made, which are then more or less perfunctorily rubber-stamped—especially in our larger cities. Intake is the court's subsystem, supposedly just screening all the cases, but in reality making many of the substantive decisions, often in a rather high-handed fashion.

Like many other professional groups, lawyers tend to vary greatly as to skill, training, expertise, honesty, commitment, capacity for helping others, and resistance to bureaucratic blandishments. Unfortunately many of the lawyers engaged in criminal practice, and in minor civil matters such as consumer debt, are quite lackluster in their training, often of dubious ethics, and the quality of their performance leaves much to be desired. On the other hand, one of the most promising programs of the Office of Economic Opportunity has been the legal services programs which attempt to deal with problems of the delivery of legal services to those who need it most. For example, the recent Supreme Court decision striking down welfare residence requirements, was in large measure due to the labors of these lawyers. Too often, legal services to the middle mass and poor are too little, and too late. For every lawyer of the "Nader's Raiders" variety there are a hundred factory-type firms such as Nixon's former law firm or the former law firm of Arnold, Fortas and Porter, which operate as subsidiary shadow governments, engaging in various forms of lobbying and influence peddling, in addition to traditional law practice.

The only other profession in which the legal system invests great hope is psychiatry. But here we find not only great variety in the quality of skills, but also a profession torn by the dissension of a multiplicity of healing faiths. Respectable psychiatric opinion no longer simply categorizes people as mentally ill or healthy, but as being located somewhere on a continuum of well—unwell, normal—abnormal. There is also increasing doubt whether the psychiatrist should even be permitted in a courtroom. A growing body of evidence indicates that our commitment procedures are haphazard, perfunctory, lacking in due process, and that there is a strong presumption of mental illness, rather than a full, objective inquiry. And more and more people no longer believe the proposition that individuals committed to mental hospitals receive the treatment for which we send them, or that a mental hospital is preferable to a prison; the reverse is true in too many instances.

There has been one promising development which may put a damper on a judge's enthusiasm for commitment as an alternative to jail. This development arises out of a New York case, Whitree vs. State 290 N. Y. Supp 2nd 693 (1968). Victor Whitree, after pleading guilty to third degree assault (a misdemeanor) in 1946, was placed on probation for three years. At some point during this period he violated probation and was sent to Bellevue hospital, where he was diagnosed as suffering from "paranoia, with alchoholism" and was committed to the (Matteawan) State Prison for the Criminally Insane in May, 1947. He remained there until September 8, 1961, at which time he was discharged. Note that Whitree had been sentenced to a *maximum* of three years on probation, but that he was confined as a result of "mental illness" for fourteen years and four months. During his entire stay at the hospital he was the subject of only one diagnostic conference (on September 10, 1947) when he was determined to be psychotic "with psychopathic personality, paranoid trends." At the time of his discharge fourteen years later, his diagnosis was the same except for the added word "improved." While incarcerated at Matteawan, Whitree was assaulted on a number of occasions by hospital employees and other inmates, he was kicked in the mouth, struck in the testicles, beaten, and hot coffee on one occasion was poured over him, causing first degree burns on his face and chest. He received numerous fractures, and several of his teeth were lost. Whitree received $300,000 in damages, because of the negligence of the state in failing to provide adequate medical care. In a harsh opinion, the court called Whitree's case the "epitome of cynicism" and his diagnosis as "improved" a "symbol of his medical and psychiatric nontreatment." This case is but one instance of a growing tide of criticism of the concept of psychiatry in the courts and of committing people for "treatment" in lieu of going to prison.

There is one final issue in connection with law and psychiatry, that of "criminal responsibility." Dr. Thomas S. Szasz has put the matter unequivocally:

Neither the M'Nagten Rule, nor the Durham Rule, nor the American Law Institute Rule is humanitarian— for all diminish personal responsibility and thus impair human dignity; nor is any of them "liberal"—for none promotes individual freedom under the rule of law. The centuries-old practice of using mental hospitalization as a means of punishing "offenders" has received fresh impetus in our day through the rhetoric of "scientific psychiatry." Contemporary concepts of "mental illness" obscure the contradictions between our pursuit of conflicting policies and objectives—individualism because it promises liberty, and collectivism because it promises security. Through the mental health ethic, psychiatry thus promotes the smooth functioning of the bureaucratic mass society and provides its characteristic ideology. According to this ideology, loss of liberty may be either punitive or therapeutic: If the individual offends because he is "bad," loss of liberty is punishment; but if he offends because he is "sick," it is therapy. From this perspective, deviance is seen as sickness rather than badness and the individual appears as a patient rather than a citizen. This is the view from the Therapeutic State.

I believe that progress in legal psychiatry now depends not on defining more and more offenders as mentally ill, but on fresh approach to the relationship between law and psychiatry. To be effective, this approach would have to clarify the dual role of psychiatry. The psychiatrist would be identified as the defender of the individual or the protector of the state. There would have to be an acknowledgement of the realities of present-day law enforcement and the public mental hospital would have to be recognized as an auxiliary of the prison system. A realistic system would have to safeguard the civil rights of the individual from psychiatry. The person would be guaranteed the same protection against loss of liberty in the mental hospital as he is against loss of liberty in prison.

We live in dangerous times and our insecurity mounts because we have failed to invest in people. There is no guarantee that the "American way of life" will survive. If the slogan of law and order is to mean anything, it must be translated into a viable system of judicial and administrative practices that operate to override the very injustices and inequities that produce the angry and desperate individuals who want to destroy the last remnants of the democratic ethic. Unless the poor and the weak, who constitute the bulk of our court and mental hospital caseload, receive the kind of protection and resources now available only to the affluent, the knowledgable and the powerful, it is useless to prate about law and order. The existing system of justice in America promotes and reinforces class warfare by indicating to those at the bottom that they have no real stake in our society. The rhetoric of law and order is a political wedge that keeps the middle mass and the rejected poor in turmoil. It engages in relentless campaigns against pasteboard villains such as marijuana and pornography, mindlessly ignoring the far greater threats posed by destruction of the environment. Unless the middle mass and the ghetto poor can surmount the specious ideological slogans of the law and order crusade, and unite in pursuit of their common social goals, America's prospects will indeed be bleak. Meaningful changes are seldom generated from within those institutions most in need of change. Our welfare, court, police, mental hospital and prison bureaucracies are in too many instances manned by a league of frightened functionaries who have been recruited in the first instance for those very features of personality and occupational socialization which are resistant to institutional change and innovation. Until more resources and personnel with fresh perspectives are committed to it, our present legal system will be the shoddy substitute for social justice, just as smog substitutes for breathable air. A nation that can mobilize its talents and resources to achieve miracles of technology, but will not invest in its own people, is in the process of destroying itself.

City University of New York   *Abraham S. Blumberg*
New York, New York

The Tipped Scales
Of American Justice

STUART S. NAGEL

The Fourteenth Amendment to the Constitution of the United States asserts that no state or local government shall "deny any person within its jurisdiction the equal protection of the laws." The due process clause of the Fifth Amendment by judicial interpretation provides a similar restraint on the federal government. Other clauses in the Bill of Rights guarantee the right to a lawyer, a grand jury indictment, a speedy trial, and a trial by jury. Do all defendants in American courts get the full benefit of these guarantees?

Many criminologists, lawyers, and other observers say that they do not. The equality before the law guaranteed by the Fourteenth Amendment often turns out in practice to be much like the equality proclaimed on George Orwell's *Animal Farm*—all men are equal, but some groups are more

A more detailed analysis of the data presented in this article may be found in Stuart S. Nagel, "Disparities in Criminal Procedure," 14 *U.C.L.A. Law Review* (1967) 1272-1305.

equal than others. Justice, some observers say, may have a blindfold, but it may also have a price, a complexion, a location, and even age and sex; and those with enough money, the right complexion, in the right court, and even sometimes of the right age and the right sex, can often get better treatment. The "least equal" in America are generally those the Fourteenth Amendment was apparently designed specifically to protect—the Negro, the poor, and the ignorant.

The Supreme Court, in an opinion in 1956, stated that "there can be no equal justice where the kind of trial a man gets depends on the amount of money he has." The Attorney General's Committee on Poverty and the Administration of Federal Criminal Justice, headed by Professor Francis A. Allen, then of the University of Michigan Law School, in its 1963 report documented the charge that the poor suffer in the courts because of their poverty. The committee recommended reforms in the bail system, in legal representation, in appeals, and at other steps in the long ladder from arrest to release or conviction.

These propositions would seem to be further supported by common sense. Bail, lawyers, appeals, parole, frequently require money and professional help which are in short supply among the poor. Policemen, prosecutors, judges, and jailors are all human products of our times and nation and, therefore, like the rest of us, are capable of error, prejudice, and "taking the easy way." Our trials are based on the adversary system, in which two more or less evenly matched sides are supposed to meet in the cockpit of a courtroom, under rules designed to insure fair play, and contend until the side with the stronger case wins. How can the indigent, the ignorant, and the victims of discrimination hope to be strong adversaries?

In answer to this question, many prosecutors, law enforcement officers, and editorial writers contend that discrimination in the administration of justice is minor and relatively unimportant. What they believe is much more important—and more damaging—is that safeguards for defendants have already thrown the scales of justice out of balance, and more safeguards could make it almost impossible to get convictions.

Perhaps the picture is muddied partly because not enough broad reliable research has been done on the American system of justice, based on a large, nationwide sample. What has been needed was an analysis of a lot of data taken at all stages of criminal procedure, from all over the country, and including both federal and state cases. This article is based on such an analysis with a concentration on grand larceny and felonious assault cases.

Disparities in justice may appear at any stage of the criminal process—and most groups suffer both apparent advantages and disadvantages from them. For instance, in larceny cases non-indigent defendants are more apt to get probation or suspended sentences than indigent ones, but are also more apt to draw longer sentences if they don't get probation, possibly because of the larger amounts of money which they steal. Also, one defendant's handicap may be another's special privilege. An adult male who does not get a grand jury hearing is possibly being denied a fundamental right; a woman or juvenile who doesn't get one is possibly being given special, informal treatment.

Let us examine these stages briefly, and see what safeguards at each level can mean to an accused.

■ PRELIMINARY HEARING. The preliminary hearing is the first stage on which data are available. The main purpose of a preliminary hearing is to allow the presiding official (police magistrate, justice of the peace, or judge) to decide whether there is enough evidence against the accused to justify further action. If he decides there is not, then an innocent person may be spared considerable humiliation, expense, delay, and inconvenience. The hearing is preliminary to the prosecutor's formal accusation or to a grand jury indictment, which it can prevent. The preliminary hearing also has other advantages for an accused: (1) it deters the use of the third-degree; (2) it allows counsel to appear and plead for the accused, particularly with regard to bail; (3) and it reveals the fact that the accused has been arrested and detained, so that *habeas corpus* (which can bring about immediate release), right to a copy of the complaint, and other guarantees can be secured. In short, the preliminary hearing is a safeguard for the rights of the accused; and its denial is a limitation to those rights.

Of the 1,168 state cases coming from counties that have provisions for preliminary hearings and on which information was available, the accused received no preliminary hearing in 434. In 357 of these he waived his right to a preliminary hearing—possibly without realizing its importance; the rest were recorded as "no preliminary hearing, reason unknown." Information as to the preliminary hearing was not available in the federal data.

■ BAIL. The next important protection for a defendant is the right, or the ability, to be released on bail. Bail reduces his hardship, especially if he is innocent, and gives him a better chance to investigate and prepare his case. Of the 1,552 state cases on which information is available, 44 percent (689) were not released on bail. Of these, 562 were eventually found guilty, 71 found not guilty, and information was not available for 56. Of the 71 not convicted, 20 had stayed in jail for two months or less, 13 for over three months, and we have no information for 38. Five of those not convicted, nor released on bail, in effect served jail terms of six months or more although found guilty of nothing.

■ DEFENSE COUNSEL. Lawyers generally concede that few persons (including lawyers) are capable of properly preparing and arguing their own cases—especially when confined. Having a lawyer, preferably of your own choice, is therefore a fundamental right.

All the state cases were felonies, punishable by more than a year in prison. Yet 183 of the 1,561 cases had no lawyer at all, and only 13 of these were recorded as having waived counsel. (Under the Supreme Court ruling in the famous case of *Gideon versus Wainright*, decided in 1963, all indigent state defendants must hereafter be assigned counsel for any felony. The 1962 data for this study, however, precedes Gideon.) In federal court, all defendants must have counsel of some kind, and the cases were divided according to whether the lawyer was the defendant's own. At least 390 of the 1,151 federal defendants did not have a lawyer of their own choosing.

A lawyer is considered essential for investigation, negotiation with the prosecutor, examination of witnesses, and the presentation of legal and factual arguments to judge and jury. A court-appointed lawyer is better than none, and often better than some, but he can easily suffer from lack of experience, sympathy, enthusiasm, and especially finances and time, since he will probably be appointed late, and may have to take much expense money out of his own pocket.

■ GRAND JURY. What percentage of cases went before a grand jury? Like the preliminary hearing (and the trial) the grand jury process is designed mainly to protect and to minimize the harm done to the innocent. The alternative is to let the prosecutor alone judge whether the accused should be held for trial. The state data did not separate those indicted by a grand jury from those who were not. Of the

915 federal cases involving either grand jury or the prosecutor alone, 344 involved only the prosecutor—although of these only half the defendants formally waived the right to a grand jury hearing.

■ DELAY. The American Law Institute Code of Criminal Procedure provides that if a defendant is held for more than three months without trial due to no fault of his own, then he must be set free without danger of rearrest for the same crime, except for extremely extenuating circumstances. A long delay before trial, especially in jail, can penalize the innocent or over-punish the guilty, as well as make witnesses less available and reliable.

The federal data unfortunately do not distinguish between those who await trial in jail and those who can afford to wait at home. Nevertheless it does reveal that, inside or out, there was, for almost half the cases, more than two months delay from arrest until release or trial (whichever came first). In the state cases, of the 405 *not* released on bail, 162 were kept in jail more than two months. (Two months was chosen as the watershed for all cases, half being delayed less, and half more.)

■ TRIAL BY JURY. Generally, there is less chance that twelve jurors will agree unanimously on conviction than one judge (especially a so-called "hanging judge"). Therefore a defendant usually has a greater chance of acquittal before a jury. In addition, if he is a member of a disadvantaged group (uneducated, working-class, or Negro) he stands a much better chance of encountering somebody like himself on a jury than on the bench.

On the other hand, our data show that seeking a jury trial may mean greater delay. It may also mean that if the defendant is found guilty, he is less likely to get probation than if he only had a bench trial. (The stiffer penalties for those convicted by juries may reflect the possibility that the more severe cases come before juries.) But on balance, the chance at a trial by "a jury of his peers" is a strong safeguard of the rights of a defendant.

Nevertheless, in the state data, 63 percent of those cases going to trial did so without a jury; 48 percent of federal trials were held without juries.

■ CONVICTION AND SENTENCING. About four of every five tried defendants, state and local, are found, or plead, guilty. The approximately 20 percent found not guilty, of course, had been put to the expense and anxiety of criminal proceedings. Of those considered guilty, 83 percent pleaded guilty—25 percent to lesser offenses than the original charge, possibly after negotiating with the prosecutor. Almost half the defendants found guilty were given suspended sentences or probation. Slightly more than half of those convicted and sentenced received sentences of more than one year.

These are the major stages in standard criminal procedure. And it is within this framework that disparities because of poverty, race, sex, age, and residence must be understood. The question is not whether the "average" accused person gets complete justice but whether some people and some groups suffer (or benefit) more or less than others—and if so, how and why.

Let us examine some of these disparities.

■ ECONOMIC CLASS. In the state data, "indigent" is defined, generally, to mean not able to afford one's own lawyer—a legalistic rather than a sociological definition. The poor, then, must usually have court-appointed lawyers, or none. In the federal cases, where indigency is not specified, the poor may be defined as those with assigned counsel.

In the pre-sentencing stages, 34 percent of indigents up for felonious assault in state courts did not get preliminary hearings—compared to 21 percent of non-indigents. This was also true, if not as markedly, in state grand larceny cases. Bail, since it requires the ability to raise money, shows the greatest disparity between those who have money and those who do not. About three-quarters of all indigent state cases did not raise bail and stayed locked up, with all this means in unearned punishment and inability to prepare for trial, while 79 percent of non-indigent assault cases, and 69 percent of larceny, did raise bail and got out.

In *having a lawyer,* an interesting reversal occurs; In most states one must be poor to have assigned lawyers, the rich hire their own, and it is the middle group that may be the most apt to be undefended. (Since the *Gideon* decision, as noted, merely having a lawyer is perhaps no longer a major disparity; what *kind* of lawyer, of course, is something else.)

In the state cases, the indigent were delayed in jail awaiting trial more than the non-indigent. This, obviously, is related to their relative inability to raise bail. In the federal figures delay is measured irrespective of whether or not the defendant is in jail—and here the indigent have *shorter* waits. A court-appointed lawyer would be inclined, apparently, to put in less time and trouble on his case than a private lawyer, and not be as apt to ask for delays; he might also want to get his bail-less client out of jail as soon as possible, and so be less likely to delay the trial.

The federal data show that the indigent are much less likely to have a grand jury indictment than the non-indigent. Perhaps they lack knowledge and are more easily persuaded to waive this right. Perhaps also this ignorance, coupled with appointed attorneys' desires to be rid of their cases, accounts for their relatively high frequency of bench, rather than jury trials. The state indigents also have proportionately fewer jury trials—but here the difference between them and the non-indigent is much less, perhaps because state juries are usually presumed to be of a lower class than federal juries, and middle-class defendants may show less preference for them.

About 90 percent of all indigents studied were found guilty. Though the percentage of non-indigents found guilty was also high, it was consistently lower (averaging about 80 percent). The greatest disparity was in the federal cases, where all indigents had court-appointed lawyers, and this may indicate that poorer representation had something to do with the higher rate of conviction. The poor also tend to feel more helpless, and may be more easily persuaded to plead guilty.

Not only are the indigent found guilty more often, but they are much less likely to be recommended for probation by the probation officer, or be granted probation or suspended sentences by the judge. Of the defendants on whom we had data in this study, a sizeable majority of indigents stayed in jail both before and after trial, unlike non-indigents.

The federal data show that this is true also of those with *no* prior record: 27 percent of the indigent with no prior record were *not* recommended for probation against 16 percent of the non-indigent; 23 percent indigent did *not* receive suspended sentences or probation against 15 percent non-indigent. Among those of both groups with "some" prior record the spread is even greater.

Why these class disparities? They reflect, at least partly, inferior legal help. But even when the lawyer works hard and well, the indigent faces the handicap that he is, and looks, lower class, while those who determine his destiny —probation officer and judge—are middle-class. Therefore, apart from the other disabilities of the poor, class bias among judicial personnel may work against them.

■ SEX. Are women discriminated against in criminal proceedings as in other walks of life? The findings are much less definite for sex than for poverty, partly because the sample was too small. (Women simply do not commit as many larcenies—and especially assaults—as men.) What differences do emerge seem to be in favor of women, especially in sentencing. It is apparently assumed that women cannot—or, chivalrously, should not—endure as much as men. On the other hand, it is possible that women can be persuaded to give up their rights more easily, and that procedures with them tend to be less formal.

Men are much less likely to be released on bail they can afford than women. In trial, women are more likely to be found innocent, and if guilty more likely to be put on probation or given suspended sentences. Studies in women's prisons have shown that women develop fewer defenses against the pains of incarceration than men and perhaps suffer more, and it is possible that judges and juries know or sense this. Or perhaps they simply find the idea of women in prison, away from their families, offensive.

■ RACE. Most Negroes are poor. A great many poor people are Negroes. So the figures about indigency and race must overlap. But they are not identical, and the differences are important. Generally, the poor suffer even more discrimination than Negroes in criminal justice; and Negroes may suffer more from lack of money than from race.

For instance, a Negro is more likely to get a preliminary hearing than a poor man. He is not as likely as the white defendant to be released on bail, but much more likely to be released than the indigent defendant. Since many Negro defendants are also indigent, the Negro is slightly more likely to have a lawyer than a white defendant, given the indigency prerequisite for receiving a court-appointed lawyer. When the Negro has a lawyer, his lawyer is much more likely to be court-appointed than the lawyers of white defendants. In the federal larceny cases, 52 percent of the

Negroes did not have their own lawyers as contrasted to 25 percent of the whites.

Like the indigent, the Negro awaiting trial with his court-appointed lawyer tends to have *less* delay than the white defendant. In fact, being subjected to delay seems to be a sign of high status rather than discrimination. Delay while released on bail may be desired by the defendant because it can benefit the guilty defendant by prolonging his freedom and weakening the memories of witnesses.

The Negro is much less likely than the white to have a grand jury indictment in either federal assault or larceny cases. If he goes to trial he is even more unlikely to have a jury trial. Indeed, 86 percent of the Negroes in federal assault cases failed to receive a jury trial, contrasted to a 26 percent figure for white defendants. It appears that the constitutional rights of a grand jury indictment and of trial by jury are mainly for white men. Perhaps Negroes believe white juries to be more discriminatory than white judges. But it is also possible that Negroes commit the less severe larcenies and assaults, and so do not as often require grand or petit juries.

Negroes, compared to whites, are particularly discriminated against when it comes to probation or suspended sentences. This is evident in the assault convictions, but is more dramatic for larceny; 74 percent of guilty Negroes were imprisoned in state larceny cases, against only 49 percent of guilty whites; in federal larceny cases the score is 54 percent to 40 percent. With prior record held constant, the disparity still holds up.

Why the difference in treatment between Negro assault and Negro larceny? Are not crimes against the person usually considered more reprehensible than those against property? The answer possibly is that larcenies by Negros are more often (than assaults) committed against white men, who are more likely to be worth robbing; but assaults occur most frequently within one's community, in this case against other Negroes. Disparities in sentencing may therefore be double, determined not only by the color of the skin of the criminal, but of his victim too.

It is interesting to note that there is a greater race disparity in federal probation *recommendations* than in probations *granted*. This may be because probation officers deal more subjectively with people, while judges (who are also better educated) tend to put more emphasis on objective factors, like the nature of the crime and the law.

On the other hand, of those actually imprisoned, the Negro defendants (particularly in larceny cases) tended to receive lighter sentences. This may be because, like the indigent defendants, they tend to steal smaller amounts; but it is probably also because the mild white offender is more likely to escape imprisonment altogether.

Generally, and surprisingly, discrimination against the Negro in criminal proceedings was only slightly greater in the South than in the North. It was, however, consistently greater in the South at all stages, pre-trial, trial, and sentencing. Discrimination in the South, predictably, was also greater at the state level than the federal level, possibly because federal judges are more independent of local pressures than state judges.

■ AGE. Younger defendants (below 21 in the state data, 22 in federal) generally are less likely to receive the safeguards the older defendants do, but are more likely to get lighter sentences.

Thus 66 percent of the young did not have their own lawyers in federal assault cases compared to 36 percent of the older defendants. They are less likely to face either grand or trial juries. There is, however, no substantial difference in preliminary hearing or bail. Much of the lack of formal procedure may actually be an advantage, reflecting a protective attitude by the courts toward the young (as toward women), and the belief that informality of procedure diminishes the "criminal" stigma, and leads more easily into rehabilitation. This is, of course, the rationale behind separate juvenile courts. The lack of a personal lawyer probably also reflects some poverty—people 21 and under seldom have much money of their own.

Young defendants are more likely to be recommended for probation, more likely to get it (or suspended sentences), and those few who do go to prison generally receive shorter sentences. (The one exception—longer sentences for youthful federal larcenists who are imprisoned—is probably unrepresentative because of the small sample, or perhaps because only the most hardened cases actually go to federal prison.) Younger people, of course, usually have shorter prior records, and this could count for some of the disparity; but the main reason is probably the belief that the young (again like women) are not as responsible, are more easily rehabilitated, and suffer more hardship in prison.

■ URBAN VS. RURAL, SOUTH VS. NORTH. The sample does not distinguish between *defendants* from the North or the South, the city or the farm—but it does distinguish between *courts* in different locales. Which were the fairest? The answer might sometimes surprise those who automatically accept the stereotype of Northern-urban civil-libertarianism, as opposed to Southern-rural anti-civil-libertarianism.

In the state data, an urban county was defined as one with more than 100,000 population; the federal data used a similar but more sophisticated definition. For both, "South" meant the original eleven states of the Confederacy. The six border states were considered neutral, and the "North" encompassed all the rest. As it developed, most cases (especially the larcenies) were tried in urban courts.

DISPARITIES IN CRIMINAL PROCEDURE TREATMENT

	DISADVANTAGED GROUPS (Indigents, Negroes, & Less Educated)	PATERNALIZED GROUPS (Juveniles & Females)	INDUSTRIALIZED GROUPS (Northern & Urban Defendants)
SAFEGUARDS FOR THE INNOCENT	Unfavorable, especially as to bail, but favorable as to being provided with a lawyer.	Unfavorable for juveniles especially as to jury trial, but unclear for females.	Unfavorable as to preliminary hearing and delay, but favorable as to providing lawyers. Mixed as to jury trial depending on the crime.
ASSAULT SENTENCING	Unfavorable, especially as to the probation officer decision.	Favorable, especially at the federal level.	Unfavorable as to whether to grant probation, but favorable as to length of imprisonment.
LARCENY SENTENCING	Unfavorable (more so than assault) as to whether to imprison, but favorable as to length of imprisonment.	Favorable, especially at the federal level.	Relatively favorable treatment.

(Based on 1,949 state cases and 981 federal cases from all 50 states for the years 1962-63 in which the defendant was charged with a single charge of assault or of larceny.)

Generally, North-South differences in treatment were greater than urban-rural differences.

In preliminary hearing and bail, urban-rural differences were small and inconclusive, but North-South differences were large and consistent—and not to the credit of the North. Thus 38 percent of Northern assaults had no preliminary hearing in spite of laws providing for them, compared to only 10 percent in the South. The South is more traditional toward law and custom, perhaps. The bail difference may also be due to the fact that more Northern defendants were classified as indigents.

Not having any lawyer at all was disproportionately rural and Southern; of the eleven Southern states, eight did not have laws providing for compensated counsel. (*Gideon vs. Wainwright* originated in a Southern state, Florida, and the South will now have to change its ways.) But in the federal cases, where assigned counsel was available, the rural and Southern defendants were *more* apt to have their own hired lawyers than in the cities and the North. That more defendants were labeled indigent in the North, and lawyers cost more there, may be an explanation.

The urban and Northern courts are more congested; defendants wait longer for trial. In the state assault cases, 56 percent of urban defendants sat in jail for more than two months, contrasted to 31 percent of rural defendants, and there is a similar 25 percent spread for federal larceny cases. Much has been written about congestion and delay in urban civil cases, but delay in criminal cases also needs attention, especially in the Northern cities.

In assault cases, jury trials and grand jury indictments are more common in the South than in the North; in larceny cases, however, it is the other way around. (The findings are similar in rural and urban courts, although not as consistent.) Urban and Northern courts are more likely to *imprison* for *assault*; the rural and Southern, for *larceny*. Perhaps these disparities reflect the "frontier" morality still lingering in the open country and the South, in which a man is expected to be prepared to personally defend his honor (and therefore assault is not so terrible) but a crime against property is something else again.

In the congested cities and the North, perhaps, crimes against the person seem more terrible, whereas property tends to be considered corporate and impersonal. Moreover, people in settled areas are more conditioned to rely on professional police, not personal defense and retribution. No great differences exist North and South, urban and rural, in percentages of convictions. But there is a good deal of difference in length of sentences. Rural and Southern courts are harsher, at least at the state level—66 percent of Southern state larceny sentences were for more than a year, contrasted to 35 percent in the North. Assault shows about the same spread. Rural-urban differences are parallel, if less marked. Southern states make the greatest use of capital punishment.

■ FEDERAL VERSUS STATE. Because of different constitutions and judicial interpretations, federal defendants have greater access to the grand jury and to counsel (when the data was collected) than state defendants. Delays are much shorter at the federal level. Shorter delays mean less need for bail, and the grand jury hearing diminishes the importance of the preliminary hearing. A slightly higher percent of federal trials are tried before juries.

Both federal and state trials end in guilty findings (or pleas) about 80 percent of the time; both find assault defendants guilty less often than larceny defendants. Probation and suspended sentences are more common in federal court—but, perhaps because the milder cases are already winnowed out, federal assault sentences are longer.

As detailed earlier, disparities unfavorable to Negroes are slightly greater in the states. Juveniles are more likely to be deprived of safeguards at the federal than the state level—but also given lighter sentences. In the broad outline, however, the same disparity patterns show up in both.

At risk of oversimplification, the major findings of this study are summarized in the accompanying chart.

Significant disparities in the administration of justice do exist. Some groups are more likely than others to receive preliminary hearings, release on bail, better lawyers, grand jury proceedings, jury trials, acquittals, shorter sentences.

Some of these differences are justifiable. The severity of the crime and the prior record, should affect the sentence (though not due process). Women and juveniles should perhaps be given more consideration. Some crimes may have greater importance in one place than another, and minor adjustments made accordingly. Nevertheless, the majority of disparities discussed in this article are probably not socially justifiable and run contrary to our democratic philosophy and to those laws which are supposed to guarantee due process and equal treatment.

What can be done about it? Remedies vary with the specific disorder. But these discriminations in the courts partly reflect the same discriminations in our society. The indigent would not get different treatment if there were no indigent; Negroes would not be discriminated against as Negroes if there were no race prejudice. If general American performance matched American oratory and promise, equality in the courts would come quickly enough. Thus the problem of criminal procedure disparities is inherently tied to attempts to remove distinctions that are considered undesirable between the city and the country and the North and the South, and to attempts to further emancipate women, as well as to decrease the numbers of the indigent and the uneducated, and to eliminate general racial discrimination.

Meanwhile, what is being done with regard to a more piecemeal attack on specific disparities?

Partly as the result of the recommendations of such groups as the Attorney General's Committee on Poverty and the Administration of Federal Criminal Justice, the Vera Foundation in New York City, and the National Bail Conference, the federal courts have been releasing many more people considered trustworthy *without bail,* pending trial. There is some evidence that state courts are starting to follow suit. Illinois now has a law requiring that most defendants waiting trial be released if they can afford a 10 percent down payment on the bail bond—the interest usually charged by commercial bondsmen. Philadelphia, New York, and St. Louis have followed the Vera recommendation to set up bodies that investigate defendants and advise judges whether they are good risks for release without bail. The fact is that judges have almost always had the authority to forego bail for trustworthy defendants— but few have been willing to use it with what little information they could pick up from the bench. In these cities at least they are using it now, and with increasing frequency.

Since *Gideon versus Wainwright,* all felony defendants can probably be assured of *some* kind of representation. In addition, a large scale campaign to provide *competent* counsel has been started by the National Legal Aid and Defender Association, and the American Bar Association. The Administrative Office of the U.S. Courts is currently conducting an educational program to encourage more rational sentencing practices and a statistical program to show more clearly just what those practices are. Though the evidence is very spotty, there does seem to be a general trend, especially in the large cities, toward better trained and better educated policemen, probation officers, and court officials. The civil rights movement, by focusing publicity on disparities, is also bringing change.

Bringing the facts to light can expedite needed change. The disparities exist partly because the facts have been denied, ignored, disbelieved, or simply unknown to a large public. The facts are available, and they keep accumulating. We may reasonably hope that when a similar study is done five or ten years from now it will show less disparity in the administration of criminal justice.

May/June 1966

Lawyers with Convictions

ABRAHAM S. BLUMBERG

The criminal trial—in a vision based not only on plays and novels, but also on a number of Supreme Court decisions—is believed to be a kind of highly civilized trial by combat. Two attorneys—one championing the people, the other championing the accused—robe themselves in the majesty of the law and battle before a stern impartial judge who considers their performances in light of the special rules of the law and grants victory to the best man.

This is a dramatic picture. But if we look closely at the reality of a large number of criminal trials, we find drama of a decidedly different kind. It may be a miracle play or a farce or a tragedy, depending on the point of view.

The defendant in a criminal court almost always loses. Most often—nine times out of ten is a good rough measure—he is found guilty. Does the prosecution have the best men, or are the police amazingly efficient? The prosecution does have good men, and the police do have competent investigators, but still we must look a little deeper to find out why losers lose.

Often, the source of their defeat has been sought in deprivations and social disabilities such as race, poverty, and social class. Researchers have attempted to learn how the deprived regard the legal system and how the system regards the deprived. But what of the legal system itself? What are the values of the judges and lawyers who work in the criminal courts? What is their thrust, purpose, and direction?

I am most concerned here with the "lawyer regulars"— those defense lawyers, including public defenders, who represent the bulk of defendants—and not with those lawyers who come to court occasionally because someone for whom they have written a will or deed has gotten into trouble. These clients end up in the hands of the regulars when their troubles are serious.

The private regulars are highly visible in the major urban centers of the nation; their offices—at times shared with bondsmen—line the back streets near courthouses. They are also visible politically, with clubhouse ties reaching into judicial chambers and the prosecutor's office. The regulars make no effort to conceal their dependence upon police, bondsmen, jail personnel, as well as bailiffs, stenographers, prosecutors, and judges. These informal relations are essential to maintaining and building a practice. Some lawyers are almost entirely dependent on such contacts to find clients, and a few even rely on an "in" with judges to obtain state-paid appointments which become the backbone of their practices.

A defense lawyer willing to go to trial can accomplish a great deal for his client, even a client technically guilty of some crime. Say the man has been arrested with a roomful of stolen furs, a satchel filled with burglar tools, a burglary record, and no alibi for the night of the crime. If the prosecution charges him with burglary, but the defense can show there was no forcible entry, then no burglary has been committed. The prosecution might try to convict on a number of lesser charges—theft, possession of stolen property, or possession of burglar tools—but in the process, the defense lawyer may have thrown up so much reasonable doubt as to get his man off. The prosecution is liable to other mistakes as well. They may have used faulty search warrants or attempted to introduce other illegal evidence; they may tamper with the witnesses or the jury; they may simply put on a bad case.

In order to accomplish these gains for his client, the defense lawyer must go to trial. However, going to trial is out of character with his role as a member of the court system. This holds true for both public and private attorneys. As members of a bureaucratic system the defense lawyers become committed to rational, impersonal goals based on saving time, labor, and expense and on attaining maximum output for the system. For the defense lawyer this means choosing strategies which will lead to working out a plea of guilty, assuring a fee, and shrouding these acts with legitimacy. The accused and his kin, as outsiders, cannot perceive the mutual dependence of the prosecutor and the defense lawyer, himself often a former prosecutor. These two need each other's cooperation for their continued professional existence. Even in bargaining over guilty pleas, their combat tends to be reasonable rather than fierce.

The defense lawyer in many ways plays the confidence man. The client is cast as the mark. The lawyer convinces him that pleading guilty will lead to a lesser charge or a lesser sentence, and the eager client agrees, forgetting that in pleading guilty, he is forfeiting his right to a trial by jury and getting a presentence hearing before a judge.

The lawyer's problem is different. He is not concerned with guilt or innocence, but rather with giving the client something for his money. Usually a plumber can show that he has performed a service by pointing to the unstopped drain or the no longer leaky faucet as proof that he merits his fee. A physician who has not performed surgery, advised a low-starch diet, or otherwise engaged in some readily discernible procedure may be deemed by the patient to have done nothing for him. Thus, doctors may order a sugar pill or water injection to overcome the patient's dissatisfaction in paying a fee "for nothing."

The practice of law has a special problem in this regard. Much legal work is intangible: a few words of advice, a telephone call, a form filled out and filed, a hurried conference with another attorney or a government official, a letter or brief, or some other seemingly innocuous or even prosaic activity. These are the basic activities, apart from any possible court appearance, of almost all lawyers at all levels of practice. The client is not looking for this, but rather for the exercise of the traditional, precise, and professional skills of the attorney: legal research and oral argument on appeals; court motions; trial work; drafting of opinions, memoranda, contracts, and other complex documents and agreements.

Despite the client's expectations, whether the lawyer has offices on Wall Street or in his hat, most legal activity more closely resembles the work of a broker, salesman, lobbyist, or agent. The product is intangible.

The members of a large-scale law firm may not speak as openly of their contacts, their fixing abilities, as does the hustling, lone-wolf lawyer. The firms trade instead upon thick carpeting, walnut paneling, genteel low pressure, and superficialities of traditional legal professionalism. There are occasions when even the large firm is defensive about the fees because the services or results do not appear substantial. Therefore, the recurrent problem in the legal profession is setting and justifying the fee.

Although the fee at times amounts to what the traffic and the conscience of the lawyer will bear, one further observation must be made about the size of the fee and its collection. The criminal defendant and his presumed loot are soon parted. Frequently the defense lawyer gets it in payment of his fee. Inevitably, the dollar value of the crime committed affects the fee, which is frequently set with precision at a sum which bears an uncanny relationship to that of the net proceeds of the crime. On occasion, defendants have been known to commit additional offenses while out on bail in order to meet their obligations for payment of legal fees. Defense lawyers teach even the most obtuse clients that there is a firm connection between paying up and the zealous application of professional expertise, secret knowledge, and organizational connections. Lawyers, therefore, seek to keep their clients at the precise emotional pitch necessary to encourage prompt fee payment. Consequently, the client treats his lawyer with hostility, mistrust, dependence, and sychophancy in precarious mixture. By keeping his client's anxieties aroused and establishing a relationship between the fee and ultimate extrication, the lawyer assures a minimum of haggling over the fee and its eventual payment.

As a consequence, all law practice in some degree involves a manipulation of the client and a stage management of the lawyer-client relationship so that there will be at least an *appearance* of help and service. At the outset, the lawyer employs with suitable variation a measure of puffery which may range from unbounded self-confidence, adequacy, and dominion over events to complete arrogance. This is supplemented by the affectation of a studied, faultless mode of personal attire. In larger firms the furnishings and office trappings will serve as the backdrop to help in impressing and intimidating the client. In all firms, solo or large scale, an access to secret knowledge and to the seats of power is implied.

The lack of a visible end product offers a special complication for the professional criminal lawyer. The plain fact is that the accused in a criminal case almost always loses, even when he has been freed by the court. All the hostility resulting from arrest, incarceration, possible loss of job, and legal expense then is directed toward the lawyer. Thus, it can also be said that the criminal lawyer never really wins a case. The really satisfied client is rare, since even vindication leaves him feeling hostile and dissatisfied. He didn't want to be arrested in the first place. Even the rare defendant who sees himself as a professional criminal and views legal fees as business expenses thinks that the overhead should be cut down. It is this state of affairs that reinforces the casting of the lawyer as a con man.

The risks of nonpayment of the fee are high. Most of the clients are poor, and most of them are likely to end up in jail, where their gratitude will be muted. It is no surprise that criminal lawyers collect their fees in advance. The fee is one of three major problems the lawyer must solve. The second is preparing the client for defeat and then cooling him out when it comes, as it is likely to do. Third, he must satisfy the court that his performance in negotiating the plea was adequate. Appellate courts are more and more looking over the trial judge's shoulder. Even the most unlikely cases may be finally decided by the Supreme Court. The next drifter accused of breaking and entering might be another Clarence Gideon.

To be sure of getting his fee, the criminal lawyer will

very often enter into negotiations with various members of the accused's family. In many instances, the accused himself is unable to pay any sort of fee or anything more than a token fee. It then becomes important to involve as many of his relatives as possible. This is especially so if the attorney hopes to collect a substantial fee. It is not uncommon for several relatives to contribute toward the fee. The larger the group, the greater the possibility that the lawyer will collect a sizable fee.

A fee for a felony case which results in a plea, rather than a trial, may range anywhere from $500 to $1,500. Should the case go to trial, the fee will be larger, depending upon the length of the trial. But the larger the fee the lawyer wishes to exact, the more impressive his performance must be. Court personnel are keenly aware of the extent to which a lawyer's stock in trade involves precarious staging of a role which goes beyond the usual professional flamboyance. For this reason alone the lawyer is bound in to the court system. Therefore, court personnel will aid the lawyer in the creation and maintenance of that impression. There is a tacit commitment to the lawyer by the court organization, apart from formal etiquette, to aid him. This augmentation of the lawyer's stage-managed image is the partial basis for the quid pro quo which exists between the lawyer and the court organization. It tends to serve as the continuing basis for the higher loyalty of the lawyer to the court organization while his relationship with his client, in contrast, is transient, ephemeral, and often superficial.

The lawyer has often been accused of stirring up unnecessary litigation, especially in the field of negligence. He is said to acquire a vested interest in a cause of action or claim which was initially his client's. The strong incentive of possible fee motivates the lawyer to promote litigation which would otherwise never have developed. The lawyers have even encoded two crimes with fine medieval names to limit this activity. *Barratry* is persistent incitement of litigation, and *champerty* is taking part in a suit without justification in exchange for a cut of the proceeds. The criminal lawyer develops a vested interest of an entirely different nature in his client's case: not to promote the litigation, but to limit its scope and duration. Only in this way can a case be profitable. Thus, he enlists the aid of relatives not only to assure payment of his fee, but to help him in his agent-mediator role of convincing the accused to plead guilty, and ultimately to help him in the "cooling out" if necessary.

It is at this point that an accused defendant may experience his first sense of betrayal. While he had perceived the police and prosecutor to be adversaries, and possibly even the judge, the accused is wholly unprepared for his counsel's role as an agent-mediator. In the same vein, it is even less likely to occur to an accused that members of his own family may become agents. Usually it will be the lawyer who will activate the family in this role, his ostensible motive being to arrange for his fee. But soon the latent and unstated motives will assert themselves. The lawyer asks the family to convince the accused to "help himself" by pleading guilty. Appeals to sentiment are exploited by a defense lawyer (or even by a district attorney) to achieve the specific end of concluding a particular matter with all possible dispatch.

The fee is often collected in installments, usually payable prior to each court appearance. In his interviews and communications with the accused or with members of his family, the lawyer employs an air of professional confidence and inside-dopesterism to assuage all anxieties. He makes the necessary bland assurances and manipulates his client, who is usually willing to do and say things, true or not, which his attorney says will help him. Since what he is selling—influence and expertise—cannot be measured by the client, the lawyer can make extravagant claims of influ- ence and secret knowledge with impunity. Lawyers fre- quently claim to have inside knowledge in connection with information in the hands of the prosecutor, police, or pro- bation officials. They often do have access to them and need only to exaggerate the nature of their relationships to im- press the client. But in the confidence game, the victim who has participated is loath to do anything which will upset the lesser plea which his lawyer has conned him into accepting.

The question has never been raised as to whether "cop- ping" a plea, or justice by negotiation, is a constitutional process. Although it has become the most central aspect of the process of criminal law administration, it has received virtually no close scrutiny by the appellate courts. As a consequence it is relatively free of legal control and super- vision. But, apart from any questions of the legality of bargaining, in terms of the pressures and devices that are employed which tend to violate due process of law, there remain ethical and practical questions. Much of the danger of the system of bargain-counter justice is concealed in secret negotiations and its least alarming feature, the final plea, is the only one presented to public view.

In effect, in his role as double agent the criminal lawyer performs a vital and delicate mission for the court organi- zation and the accused. Both principals are anxious to terminate the litigation with a minimum of expense and damage to each other. There is no one else in the court structure more strategically located or more ideally suited to handle this than the defense lawyer. In recognition of this, judges will cooperate with attorneys in many important ways. For example, they will continue the case of an accused in jail awaiting plea or sentence if the attorney requests it. This may be done for some innocuous and seemingly valid public reason, but the real purpose is pressure by the attorney for the collection of his fee, which he knows he may lose if the case is concluded. Judges know of this none too subtle method of dunning a client. The judges will go along on the ground that important ends are being served. Often, however, the only end being served is to protect a lawyer's fee.

Another way the judge can help an accused's lawyer is by lending the official aura of the bench as a backdrop to an all-out performance for the accused in justification of his fee. The judge and other court personnel will serve as supporting players for a dramatic scene in which the defense lawyer makes a stirring appeal in his behalf. With a show of restrained passion, the lawyer will intone the virtues of the accused and recite the social deprivations which have reduced him to his present state. The speech varies somewhat, depending on whether the accused has been convicted after trial or has pleaded guilty. The incongruity, superficiality, and ritualistic character of the performance is underscored by a visibly impassive, almost bored reaction on the part of the judge and other members of the court retinue. Afterward there is a hearty exchange of pleasantries between the lawyer and district attorney, wholly out of the context of the adversary nature of the hearing. The courtroom players are not "method" actors.

The fiery passion of the defense is gone, and lawyers for both sides resume their offstage relations, chatting amiably and perhaps even including the judge in their restrained banter. Even a casual observer is put on notice; these individuals have claims upon each other.

Criminal law practice is unique since it really only appears to be private practice but is actually bureaucratic practice. Private practice is supposed to involve an organized, disciplined body of knowledge and learning. Individual practitioners are imbued with a spirit of autonomy and service. Earning a livelihood is incidental. But the lawyer in the criminal court serves as a double agent, serving organizational rather than professional ends. To some extent the lawyer-client confidence game serves to conceal this fact.

The "cop-out" ceremony is not only invaluable for redefining the defendant's perspectives of himself, but also in reiterating his guilt in a public ritual. The accused is made to assert his guilt of a specific crime, including a complete recital of its details. He is further made to say that he is entering his plea of guilty freely and that he is not doing so because of any promises that may have been made to him. This last is intended as a blanket statement to shield the court bureaucrats from any charges of coercion. This cuts off any appellate review on grounds that due process was denied as well as cutting off any second thoughts the defendant may have about his plea.

This affirmation of guilt is not a simple affair. Most of those who plead guilty are guilty and may be willing or even eager to say so in order to be charged with a lesser crime or receive a lesser sentence. The system serves the guilty better because they are glad to get half a loaf in return for playing along. But the innocent—subject to precisely the same pressures—get no reward from a negotiated plea. In any case, the defendant's conception of himself as guilty is ephemeral; in private he will quickly reassert his innocence. The "cop-out" is not comparable to Harold Garfinkel's "status degradation ceremony" because it has no lasting effect on the interrelations of the defendant and society. Rather, it is a charade. The accused projects the appropriate amount of guilt, penance, and remorse; his hearers engage in the fantasy that he is contrite and merits a lesser punishment.

Defendants begin dropping the guilty role very soon. Many do so in their interviews with the probation officer immediately after the plea but before sentencing. The first question the probation officer routinely asks is: "Are you guilty of the crime to which you pleaded?" I have gathered the responses of 724 male defendants to this question. The research was done in 1962, 1963, and 1964 in a large metropolitan court handling only felonies. The men were charged with crimes ranging from homicide to forgery, but most of them pleaded guilty to misdemeanors after negotiation. At this early stage, 51.4 percent claimed innocence in some fashion. In practice when a prisoner claims innocence, the probation officer will ask him to withdraw his plea and stand trial on the original charges. This threat is normally sufficient to provide the system with a second affirmation of guilt.

Very few choose to go on trial again. They are very likely to be convicted if they do. Between 1950 and 1964 in the court I studied, from 75 to 90 percent of the actual adversary trials ended in conviction. In all years less than 5 percent of all indictments ended in adversary trials.

In the present system it would appear that once an individual is indicted, there is very little chance of escaping conviction.

The unrehearsed responses to the probation officer tell us a great deal about how defendants feel about their negotiated pleas. Only 13.2 percent straightforwardly admitted their guilt and of these, 10.3 percent added exculpatory statements such as, "But I should have gotten a better deal (from the lawyer, prosecutor, police, judge)." The large group claiming innocence, 373 men, were for the most part interested in underscoring their "goodness" for the probation officer.

These innocent respondents employed varying degrees of fervor, solemnity, and credibility. In the main they were pragmatic, saying, "I wanted to get it over with," or "You can't beat the system," or "They have you over a barrel when you have a record." This pragmatic response covered 20.3 percent of the sample. "I followed my lawyer's advice," was the claim of 12.7 percent. Nearly as many defendants—11.8 percent—said they had been manipulated or conned by lawyer, judge, police, or prosecutor. The smallest number—2.1 percent—traced their plea to a "bad report" by the probation officer or psychiatrist in investigations before hearing the plea. Only a very few were defiant outright; just 4.5 percent (or 33) claimed that they had been framed or betrayed.

By far the largest grouping in the sample were those who were fatalistic, neither pressing their innocence nor admitting their guilt. This 34.8 percent (248) explained their pleas by saying, "I did it for convenience," or "My lawyer told me it was the only thing I could do," or "I did it because it was the best way out." This last group seemed to feel that they, like Joseph K. in Kafka's *The Trial*, are caught up in a monstrous apparatus which may turn on them no matter what they do, no matter whether they say they are innocent or guilty. These men adopt a stance of passivity, resignation, and acceptance. Interestingly, in most instances it was their lawyer who crystallized the alternatives for them and who was therefore the critical element in their decision to plead guilty.

In order to determine the critical elements in all 724 cases, the men were asked who first suggested the plea of guilty and who most influenced their final decision to enter this plea. The results are listed in Table I:

TABLE I—DECISIONS TO PLEAD GUILTY

Agent-Mediator	First Suggestion		Most Influence	
	No.	%	No.	%
Judge	4	0.6	26	3.6
Prosecutor	67	9.3	116	16.0
Defense counsel	407	56.2	411	56.8
Probation officer	14	1.9	3	0.4
Psychiatrist	8	1.1	1	0.1
Wife	34	4.7	120	16.6
Friends and relatives	21	2.9	14	1.9
Police	14	1.9	4	0.6
Fellow inmates	119	16.4	14	1.9
Others	28	3.9	5	0.7
No response	8	1.1	10	1.4

It is popularly assumed that most guilty pleas are a result of pressure to confess from the police or more elaborate coercion from the prosecutor. In my sample, however, only 43 men, or 5.94 percent, had confessed before they were indicted, and as Table I shows, the defense attorney was by far the most potent source of guilty pleas, particularly if it is recalled that most of the pressure from family and friends to plead this way is likely to be generated by the defense attorney. The bureaucratic system cannot rely on idiosyncratic police pressures for confessions and retain its efficiency, high production, and rational-legal character. The defense counsel is a far more effective source of pleas, living as he does astride the world of the court and the world of the defendant. Even though fellow inmates were frequently the first to mention such a plea, defendants still tended to rely strongly on their counsel as the ultimate source of influence for a final decision.

Therefore, I asked the 724 defendants at what point in their relationship the defense counsel first suggested a guilty plea. Although these men cited many sources of influence, they all had lawyers, and of course they were not likely to plead without concurrence by or at least consultation with their lawyers. In the court I studied there are three basic kinds of defense counsel: private, legal-aid (a private defender system which receives public funds and has taken on the coloration of a public defender system), and court-assigned (who may later be privately retained).

The overwhelming majority related a specific incident of an early suggestion that they plead guilty to a lesser charge if this could be arranged. Of all the agent-mediators, it is the lawyer who is most effective in manipulating the defendant, notwithstanding possible pressures by police, prosecutor, judge, or others. Legal-aid and assigned counsel

TABLE II—STAGE AT WHICH PLEA WAS FIRST
SUGGESTED OR DISCUSSED

Meeting	Private	Legal-Aid	Assigned	All	%
First	66	237	28	331	45.7
Second	83	142	8	233	32.2
Third	29	63	4	96	13.3
Fourth or later	12	31	5	48	6.6
No response	0	14	2	16	2.2
TOTAL NUMBER OF CASES	190	487	47	724	100.0%

are apparently more likely to suggest the plea in the initial interview, perhaps as a response to pressures of time and, in the case of the assigned counsel, the strong possibility that there is no fee involved. In addition, there is some further evidence in Table II of the perfunctory character of criminal courts. Little real effort is made to individualize the defendant. Although the defense lawyer is an officer of the court he mediates between the court organization and the defendant; his duties to each are rent by conflicts of interest. Too often these must be resolved in favor of the organization which provides him with his professional existence. In order to reduce the strains and conflicts imposed, the lawyer engages in the lawyer-client confidence game so as to make his situation more palatable.

Based on data which are admittedly tentative and fragmentary, the furor over confessions, whether forced or voluntary, is not statistically meaningful. Criminal law enforcement has always depended, and will continue to do so in the foreseeable future, on judicial confessions—that is, pleas of guilty—rather than confessions hammered out in the squeal room of a police station.

The Gideon, Miranda, and Escobedo decisions were greeted with such lively delight or anguished dismay that outsiders must have thought that the Supreme Court had wrought some magnificent transformation in the defense lawyer. Actually, the court in these cases was perpetuating the Perry Mason myth of an adversary trial, while in the lesser courts of the nation, the dreary succession of 90 percent negotiated pleas continued. These "trials" are highly reminiscent of what George Feifer described in *Justice in Moscow*. The Soviet trial has been termed "an appeal from the pre-trial investigation." All notions of the presumption of innocence are completely alien, and as Feifer states: ". . . the closer the investigation resembles the finished script, the better. . . ."

I do not mean to be pejorative. Feifer finds the Soviet trial preferable in some ways because it judges the criminal and not the crime, but in the American form, the "irrelevant" factors of background and record are considered only after the finding of guilty, not before as in Russia and much of Europe.

The Escobedo and Miranda decisions protecting against defendant confusion in the hands of the police and the

Gideon decision assuring counsel for felony defendants are popular in and out of legal circles, but my experiences and observations suggest that a poor defendant with a lawyer may not be much better off than a poor defendant without a lawyer. These decisions have not changed the nature of the court bureaucracy and, if anything, the pressure for guilty pleas and the drive for efficient production may grow even stronger, and the position of the defendant as a bureaucratic client further hampered by race, poverty, and class may become weaker and weaker.

Courts, like many other large modern organizations, possess a monstrous appetite not only for individuals, but for entire professions. Almost all those coming under an organizational authority find their definitions, perceptions, and values have been refurbished in terms largely favorable to the particular organization and its goals.

Thus, the Supreme Court decisions extending the right to counsel may have an effect which is radically different from that intended or anticipated. The libertarian rules will tend to augment the existing organizational arrangements, enriching court organizations with more personnel and elaborate structure, and making them an even more sophisticated apparatus for processing defendants toward a guilty finding.

July/August 1967

Winners and Losers...
Garishment and Bankruptcy
In Wisconsin

HERBERT JACOB

The prospect of being dragged into court for not paying one's debts or else pleading bankruptcy in order to evade them looms in the future of thousands of Americans every year. But whether the courts will be the last resort of debt collectors and debt dodgers depends on numerous influences ranging from the attitude of individual communities regarding indebtedness to the life-styles of debtors and creditors.

The courts are the most important contact many citizens have with the government. But whether this political instrument is used to seize wages of those owing money or to help others evade payment by declaring them bankrupt is related to income, the type of debt incurred, job status, to some degree race, and the manner in which the community where the action is taking place views itself.

To find out who uses the courts for garnishment and bankruptcy proceedings, we searched the court records of

69

four Wisconsin cities—Madison, Racine, Kenosha, and Green Bay. In Green Bay, where the number of such proceedings was small, all debtor-creditor cases for a year were recorded. A random sample was taken from the other cities' files.

In all, 454 debtors were interviewed. Another 336 creditors and 401 employers returned completed questionnaires. Interviews with selected attorneys, creditors, collection agencies, and court officials added to the information. From these sources emerged profiles of creditors and debtors and their use of the courts.

Debtor-creditor conflicts usually involve the refusal of the debtor to pay what the creditor feels is due him. The debtor may feel he was cheated or that the creditor didn't live up to the agreement. Unemployment, ill health, a family emergency, or pressure from other creditors to repay them first are other common reasons that people don't pay bills. Sometimes, the debtor simply forgets or no longer wants to pay. In each case, the probability of conflict is high, for most creditors pursue the debtor until he pays. Only when collection costs rise above the amount owed, will most creditors write off the loss.

The typical creditor is a finance company, department store, service station, television repair shop, landlord, hospital, doctor, or even lawyer. A few creditors are personally involved insofar as they themselves extend credit, lend money, or have extensive personal relations with their customers and make a personal effort to collect the loan. Most collectors do not make loans, but are employees of large collection organizations and view collecting as a routine matter.

When most private actions to collect debts fail, the courts stand ready to help creditors: (1) If an article were purchased through a conditional sales contract, the creditor may repossess, sell it, and get a deficiency judgment for the difference between the resale price and the amount still owed on the item from the debtor. (2) The creditor may obtain a judgment so that he can use the sheriff's office in collecting the amount due. The sheriff can seize for sale any articles not exempt under the state law. (3) When, as in many cases, the debtor owns no goods that satisfy the judgment, most states allow the creditor to attach the debtor's wages through wage garnishment. In some states like Wisconsin, creditors may seize the debtor's wages through garnishment even before they obtain a judgment against the debtor.

Under garnishment proceedings, a summons is sent to the debtor's employer, who is then obligated to report whether he owes the debtor any wages. If he does, he must send those wages to court. The debtor may recover some of his wages for living expenses but the bulk of the funds satisfies the debt. A creditor may garnishee his debtor's wages repeatedly until the debt is paid.

Debtors, in turn, have a number of extralegal remedies they can use. In a country where there is free movement and different state laws regarding creditor-debtor relations, the easiest thing for a debtor to do may be to move. Or he may defend his nonpayment in the judgment suit, though this is expensive and rarely successful. But debtors increasingly use a more successful legal measure—promising repayment through a court-approved amortization plan.

Such plans may be available under state law (as in Wisconsin) or through Chapter 13 of the Federal bankruptcy statute. Under the Wisconsin statute, a debtor earning less than $7,500 per year may arrange to repay his debts in full within two years if his creditors consent. During this time, he is protected from wage garnishments and other court actions that seek to collect the debts listed. New debts, however, may be collected as before through judgments or wage garnishments. Under Chapter 13 of the Bankruptcy Act, amortization usually allows the debtor three years to pay. During this time, interest accumulation is stopped and all creditor actions against the debtor are prohibited. New debts as well as old ones may be included in the repayment plan although new debts may be incurred only with the approval of a court-appointed trustee. Chapter 13 also provides for partial payment in satisfaction of the debt.

Bankruptcy provides the final legal escape for the debtor. Bankruptcy is available under Federal law to both the business and nonbusiness debtor. A debtor need not be penniless; he only needs to have debts which he cannot pay as they fall due. Under bankruptcy proceedings, the debtor makes available to the court all nonexempt assets that he possesses for repayment to his creditors.

Nonbusiness bankruptcies usually involve no assets that can be distributed to creditors. After this has been established, the Federal court discharges the debts of the bankrupt and he is no longer legally obligated to repay. (Tax debts, alimony, and child support payments as well as debts incurred through fraud cannot be discharged.) The only limitation to this remedy for debtors is that it may be used only once every six years.

Only a tiny proportion of credit transactions turn into conflicts between creditor and debtor and only a small proportion of those are eventually brought to court. It is therefore important to identify the conditions under which some people seek to invoke governmental sanctions in their efforts to collect or evade debts. *Four sets of conditions* are readily identifiable and are the subject of analysis here.

■ *Socioeconomic conditions:* A recession (even if slight and local) following a period when credit was freely extended is likely to produce more creditor-debtor conflicts than continued prosperity or a long recession. Likewise, the type of economy in an area is important. Subsistence economies, either in rural or urban slums, do not involve much consumer credit. Factory workers whose employment or earnings are erratic are more likely to be in credit difficulties than white-collar workers whose employment is steadier and whose wages, although lower, are more regular. The availability of credit is also significant. Those living in small towns or cities with few banks and lending institutions may find it more difficult to get credit and also find themselves less tempted to borrow than those living amidst a plethora of lending institutions, constantly inviting them to borrow.

■ *"Civic"* or *"public"* culture of a community: Some communities have more conservative lending policies than others. Large blocs of citizens may not borrow because they are older and not used to it or because they come from ethnic groups unaccustomed to living on credit. Alternatively, some communities are composed of groups who borrow heavily. In some communities, using the courts comes easily; in others, it involves a morally and culturally difficult decision.

■ *Availability of court action:* In some communities, court action is unlikely because no court sits in the town—all actions must be started in a distant town making litigation inconvenient as well as expensive. Also, some courts are more stringent about requiring representation by lawyers than others. In one town, attorneys may be more available for collection work than in others. Finally, litigation costs vary from town to town, as local judges interpret state laws regarding fees in different ways.

■ *Ability of potential litigants to use remedies:* Different members of a community vary considerably in their ability to use available remedies. They need to know about them.

They need the requisite financial resources. They need to be convinced that court action is really appropriate in their situation and to be free of the psychological restraint of shame and the social restraint of retaliation.

In the cities studied, money lenders (principally finance companies), and retailers were the heaviest users of wage garnishments. Hospitals, doctors, and dentists were the third most frequent users in three cities, while in the fourth, landlords were. All other creditors accounted for less than one-third of the wage garnishments docketed in small-claims court.

Creditors, however, do not use wage garnishments in identical ways. Their readiness to use the courts occurs under very different conditions. Finance companies, for example, have the most developed collection system. Ten days after a payment is due, they consider the debtor delinquent and begin efforts to collect. A large repertoire of collection methods are called into play, including overdue notices, telephone calls to the debtor, personal calls to his home, telephone calls to his employer, calls to co-signers of his note (if any), seizure of the collateral for the loan (if any), and wage garnishment. Most of these steps are carried out with minimal assistance by outsiders since their internal organization is structured to accommodate them. Consequently, finance companies almost never use collection agencies. And although they garnishee frequently, they do so only after a long chain of attempts to collect.

Doctors and hospitals are in a different position. Medical ethics downgrade commercial success, and patients reinforce this de-emphasis. Most patients expect a bill; few expect a bill collector to follow. Medical services are something they feel entitled to, regardless of their ability to pay, and therefore even when medical clinics and hospitals have business offices, they do not usually use them for extensive bill-collecting purposes.

Most doctors are not organized for nor do they depend on credit profits. Yet collectively, they probably extend as much credit as finance companies do. As professionals, they dislike spending time collecting delinquent bills. Generally, they wait three months before they consider a bill delinquent. They then send one or two reminders to the patient. They do not call him at home or at work. They have no co-signer through whom to exert pressure; they have no purchases to repossess. They do not even have the time to go to court themselves, so they usually turn delinquent accounts over to a collection agency or attorney. One or two more impersonal attempts are made to collect before the issue goes to court for a judgment and/or wage garnishment. Typically, the doctor and the hospital receive only half the proceeds collected by the agency, the other half being the agency's fee. Most maintain that they pay little attention to what the collection agency does to collect a bill and are unaware that they are garnisheeing their patients' wages. Some say they resort to collection agencies for tax reasons only, since they believe the Internal Revenue Service does not permit them to write off a delinquent account as uncollectable unless court action was attempted.

Retail merchants stand between finance companies and medical men in their use of wage garnishments. Large stores with thousands of accounts have about the same organizational capability of collecting debts as finance companies. Small merchants have to use collection agencies. Like doctors, most retailers do not consider accounts delinquent until 90 days after payment is due and they also have no collateral to repossess since most retail sales are for soft goods. When hard goods such as TVs and refrigerators are sold on credit, the notes are sold by the retailer to a finance company. Retailers, moreover, are sensitive to their customers' opinions of them. Nearly 25 percent of the retailers interviewed were afraid that if they were frequently involved in direct wage garnishments they would lose customers. Almost 50 percent of the doctors expressed similar fears, but no finance company and very few banks and credit unions mentioned this as a reason for not using garnishments more often.

Willingness to use government help in collecting delinquent accounts thus seems to depend, in part, on the organizational resources of creditors, on their dependence on credit for profits, and on restraints produced by customer or patient alienation. Finance companies frequently use the courts because they possess the organizational resources, depend entirely on credit profits, and have little to fear since their customers generally have no other place to borrow. Doctors, hospitals, and retailers differ on all these points from finance companies and, insofar as they differ, are less likely to use the courts. Many, however, are indirectly drawn into court actions by the collection agencies they employ because collection agencies have the same characteristics as finance companies: the organizational resources to sue, their existence depends on collecting, and they have no fear of customer alienation.

The size of the debt is another important variable in the use of the courts. Most bills leading to wage garnishments are relatively large. Only 16 percent involved less than $50. Most were $50-$99, the median was $100-$149. About 20 percent were between $400 and $500, the upper limit of small-claims actions.

Most creditors find that costs are too high for debts of less than $50 to risk wage garnishment proceedings. It costs up to $35 (half in court fees and half in attorney's fees) to collect a bill by garnishment. If the creditor is successful in assessing the garnishment, the debtor pays the court fees. But if the garnishment is unsuccessful—if the creditor puts the wrong employer down on the summons or if he garnishes when the employer does not owe his employee any wages (for example, the day *after* payday rather than the day before)—the creditor must pay the full costs.

Since most debtors earn less than $100 a week, most debts far exceed the amount that can be collected by a single garnishment. Under Wisconsin law, the employer must usually pay the debtor $25 if he is single and $40 if he has dependents before he turns wages over to the court for payment to the creditor. Thus, most garnishments capture $60 or less out of which both the original debt and the court and attorney fees must be paid. In many cases it would take at least three garnishments to satisfy the debt and few debtors are likely to remain on their job beyond two such proceedings. Either they are fired because of the garnishments or quit in order to escape them. Most creditors therefore use wage garnishment to force the debtor to come in and make an arrangement to repay more gradually. As we shall see later, however, these generalizations about the users of garnishment proceedings are not entirely accurate for every city studied, with the locale making a considerable difference.

While creditors are often organizations, the debtors we studied were always individuals. Bankrupts had most often purchased large items such as cars (generally, used cars), appliances, TVs, furniture, and encyclopedias in the three years before going bankrupt. Garnishees, however, reported such purchases far less frequently, mentioning only two luxury items with consistency—home freezers and air conditioners. Medical debts were common to all; 82 percent of the bankrupts and 92 percent of the garnishees reported they were behind in their medical bills. Garnishees were more often protected by medical insurance. While 84 percent said some of their medical bills were paid by insurance, only 66 percent of the Chapter 13's and 57 percent of the bankrupts had similar protection.

Significantly, debtors in our sample who sought court relief were very similar to those who did not. Although

Table I

INDEBTEDNESS OF BANKRUPTS, CHAPTER 13's AND GARNISHEES

Indebtedness	Bankrupts *(N = 196)	Chapter 13's (N = 72)	Garnishees (N = 168)
Up to $999	.5	9.7	25.6
$1000-4999	56.6	73.6	52.4
$5000-9999	20.4	12.4	10.1
Over $10000	22.9	4.2	11.9
* Number of cases			

garnishees generally had a lower level of indebtedness, and many bankrupts were hopelessly mired in the quicksand of credit, most owed about the same amount of money —between $1,000 and $5,000. (See Table I)

■ Slightly more than half the bankrupts had incomes below $6,000, less than the median family income for the four Wisconsin cities in 1959. Like the garnishees, the vast majority were above the official "poverty" line of $3,000. Most of the Chapter 13's and garnishees reported incomes above $6,000. (See Table II) The most striking difference between the three groups is the frequency of home ownership, with garnishees owning homes more often. This difference may in part be attributed to the loss of homes by bankrupts in the bankruptcy proceedings.

■ As Table III indicates, garnishees who did not go

through bankruptcy court often had larger numbers of wage garnishments levied against them than did bankrupts or Chapter 13's. In fact, many of the bankrupts and Chapter 13's reported neither actual garnishment nor threatened garnishment prior to court relief from their debts.

What then distinguishes those who seek government aid to evade debts from those who don't? Indebtedness and assets do not clearly differentiate the three groups, nor do education and occupation. Most debtors, 84 percent to 87 percent, had at least some high-school education. Most were blue-collar workers—craftsmen, foremen, factory workers, or laborers. A small proportion, ranging from 10 percent of the Chapter 13's to 15 percent of the bankrupts were white-collar workers.

Age, however, separates the three groups. Younger debtors go bankrupt more frequently than older ones. Sixty-two percent of the bankrupts were less than 30 years old. Only 43 percent of the Chapter 13's and 37 percent of the gar-

Table II

SELECTED ASSETS OF DEBTORS:
TOTAL FAMILY INCOME, HOME OWNERSHIP

Income	Bankrupts	Chapter 13's	Garnishees
Less than $3000	6.2%	6.1%	5.4%
$3000-5999	47.4%	30.7%	33.9%
$6000-9999	40.7%	57.0%	48.2%
Over $10000	5.7%	6.1%	12.5%
Number of cases	209	65	168
Home Ownership			
Own or buying	21.2%	36.4%	42.1%
Number of cases	212	66	171

nishees were so young. *A majority of the bankrupts were young men in the early years of their family life who had built up high levels of debt, purchasing most of the items needed to establish a household.* Most did not have more than two children living with them. By contrast, the garnishees were a much older group with well-established homes; often their children had already left home so that they too were usually supporting households with two children or less.

Moreover, a relatively high proportion of the debtors were Negroes. While only 2.5 percent of the total population were black, 16 percent of the garnishees, 12 percent of the Chapter 13's, and 9 percent of the bankrupts were Negroes. This is not surprising given the generally high

Table III

ACTUAL AND THREATENED GARNISHMENT

Actual Garnishment	Bankrupts	Chapter 13's	Garnishees
None	44.3%	45.3%	—
1-2	28.8%	22.7%	58.1%
3-5	15.6%	17.3%	30.4%
More than 5	11.3%	14.6%	11.5%
Number of cases	214	75	174
Threatened Garnishment			
Yes	55.6%	72.7%	50.3%
Number of cases	214	77	176

income of Negroes in the four cities and the likelihood that Negroes are more tempted to overpurchase, because of their previously deprived status and because of the hard-sell techniques. That fewer Negroes take advantage of court relief from their debts results from their being among the least efficacious members of society and that they may know courts only from criminal proceedings.

Neither indebtedness, income, education, nor age distinguish Negroes who seek court relief from debts from those who don't. The difference is principally occupational status, with craftsmen and foremen going to bankruptcy court and mainly factory workers being garnished.

A number of characteristics seemingly related to the occupational status of Negroes are present among the whole sample of debtors. High-job status Negroes are relatively well-integrated at their work place and probably better integrated into the general community than lower-occupation status Negroes. Furthermore, they are probably better linked in communication networks through which they may learn about bankruptcy than are lower-status Negroes. These inferences can't be tested here because the number of Negroes in the sample is too small for more detailed analysis. But these hypotheses should also hold true for the entire group of debtors.

The data indicate that there are significant differences between garnishees and bankrupts in the quantity of information they had and the direction of advice they received about their financial distress. Bankrupts were apparently much better integrated into the legal system than garnishees since twice as many bankrupts as garnishees saw an attorney about a previous garnishment. In addition, those who saw an attorney in the two groups received different advice. Only half the bankrupts were advised to make arrangements to pay their creditors while 75 percent of the garnishees were given that advice. More than 40 percent of the bankrupts were advised by their attorney to go into bankruptcy; less than 20 percent of the garnishees received such advice. Combining the effects of the propensity to see a lawyer and the advice lawyers gave, we find that almost half of the bankrupts were told to take advantage of bankruptcy, while only 5 percent of the garnishees received such advice from a lawyer.

Bankrupts also received different advice from their friends than the garnishees. Far fewer bankrupts reported that their friends advised "doing nothing" or paying their creditors off. Many more reported being advised to see an attorney about their garnishment and a significant proportion (17 percent) were told about bankruptcy, whereas not a single garnishee reported being told about bankruptcy by a friend.

Other data also indicate the importance of integration into a communication network which facilitates the decision to go into bankruptcy. The second most frequent response to "Why did you decide to go into bankruptcy?" was advice from various quarters—most often that advice came from their attorney. In addition, when we asked them where they learned about bankruptcy, lawyers were the most frequently mentioned source of information. Friends, relatives, and people at their place of work followed. The overwhelming proportion of our sample learned about bankruptcy from personal sources rather than from impersonal communications. Indeed, the media were not specifically mentioned by a single one of the almost 200 bankrupt respondents. A final indicator of the importance of personal communications comes from the fact that more than half the bankrupts knew someone else who had gone through bankruptcy.

These data indicate that bankrupts were integrated into the legal system by a communication network which was conversant with bankruptcy proceedings. Although bankrupts varied greatly in their socioeconomic characteristics, they were linked in a loose communication network. They apparently learned about bankruptcy with relative ease and received support from the various people from whom they heard about bankruptcy. All of this contrasts sharply with the experience of garnishees. Garnishees, although in financial difficulty, were shut out of that network. Thus they did not learn about bankruptcy, were not encouraged to use it, and were not in contact with the professionals who might facilitate their use of it.

Neither creditors nor debtors used the courts to the same extent in the four cities studied. Nor did the variation in

Table IV

GARNISHMENT AND BANKRUPTCY ACTIONS
FOR 12 MONTH PERIOD:

	Madison	Racine	Kenosha	Green Bay
Garnishments	2860	2740	813	130
per 1000 pop.	22.6	30.7	12.0	2.1
Bankruptcies	112	100	63	32
Chapter 13's	37	18	5	7
Total BK-13 per 1000 pop.	1.17	1.32	1.0	.62

garnishment and bankruptcy rates in the four cities conform to social, economic, or partisan factors. (See Table IV) Each of the cities had approximately the same degree of prosperity during the period studied. The proportion of families with incomes in the range where garnishment and bankruptcy most frequently occurs ($3,000-$10,000) was almost identical for Madison, Racine, and Kenosha. Green Bay had slightly more such families but this scarcely explains its *lower* garnishment and bankruptcy rate. All cities had small nonwhite populations. Racine has the largest Negro community consisting of 5.4 percent of its population. Only .9 percent of Green Bay's population was nonwhite, principally Indian. And though there are no available figures on the amount of credit extended in the four cities, the differences in retail sales for the four do not explain the differences in garnishment and bankruptcy rates.

The only factor clearly explaining the different rates of garnishment and bankruptcy in the four cities might be called the "public" or "legal" culture. Excluding garnishment and bankruptcy, the frequency with which civil court cases are initiated in the four cities closely follows debtor case rates. (See Table V) The highest rate occurs in Racine, with Madison, Kenosha, and Green Bay following. As expected, the criminal rates differ since they are initiated by public officials. Civil cases, for the most part, are initiated by private citizens. All civil litigation reflects, it then seems, a set of peculiar institutional and cultural patterns that are not evident in the standard socioeconomic indexes ordinarily applied to these cities.

Robert Alford and Harry M. Scoble's study of these four cities and their municipal decision-making processes

Table V

CIVIL AND CRIMINAL CASES IN FOUR COUNTIES, JULY 1, 1964-JULY 1, 1965

Civil Cases	Dane (Madison)	Racine	Kenosha	Brown (Green Bay)
County and Circuit Court	1691	817	1203	803
Small Claims Court (minus garnishment)	4203	3024	743	233
Civil Case Rate 1000 pop.	26.5	27.0	19.5	8.2
Criminal Cases (excluding ordinance)	3195	1020	867	722
Rate/1000 pop.	15.8	7.2	8.6	5.8

suggests that they represent distinct political cultures. They label these cultures as (1) *traditional conservatism* (Green Bay), government is essentially passive, a caretaker of law and order, not an active instrument for social or private goals; (2) *traditional liberalism* (Kenosha), "the bargaining process may even extend to traditional services . . .;" (3) *modern conservatism* (Racine), government is legitimately active, but furthering private economic interests that are in the long range public interest, and (4) *modern liberalism* (Madison), "a high level of political involvement . . . may itself exacerbate conflicts. . . ." Alford and Scoble concentrate on the liberal-conservative dimensions of the four cities, by focusing on the kinds of public decisions made and the range of participation in the decision-making process. When we examine litigation rates, however, the cities cluster on the traditional-modern dimension. It appears that Green Bay and Kenosha share low litigation rates because of more traditional public cultures, while Racine and Madison share higher litigation rates because of their more modern public culture. Data from our interviews provide supporting evidence for this conclusion.

Less frequent use of public facilities to settle private conflicts is congruent with the concept of a traditional American public culture. Depending more on personal and less on bureaucratic ways of settling disputes, the traditional culture leads to dependence on personal contact between the principals.

Taking a debtor to court is a highly impersonal proceeding involving the use of public officials as intermediaries and arbiters. Interview data indicate that in Green Bay and Kenosha firms and professionals collecting delinquent accounts depend more on the use of personal contacts, telephone calls to the debtor, or informal arrangements with employers. In Green Bay, where the garnishment rate is lowest, attorneys and creditors often asserted that the city was small enough for everyone to know everyone else, making court action unnecessary. But Green Bay has only 5,000 fewer inhabitants than Kenosha (where no respondents mentioned the intimacy of the town) and is only one-third smaller than Racine which has the highest garnishment rate. Nevertheless, the exaggeration of its small size is significant, since the perception of Green Bay as a small town fits the description of its traditional culture.

The lower garnishment rate also fits Alford's description of these traditional cities as ones in which the business elite does not look upon government as an instrument to obtain private objectives. Passive government and informal bargaining typify many public situations in Green Bay and Kenosha, with the debt-collection process being just one manifestation. In Madison and Racine, creditor-debtor conflicts, like public disputes, more frequently reach official government agencies—in this case, the court—for formal adjudication.

Alford's characterization of these cities leads us to look for differences in the degree to which the people are fiscally traditional.

For the most part, these expectations are confirmed by the debtor interviews. Slightly more debtors in Green Bay than elsewhere thought banks were the best place to borrow money and an overwhelming proportion thought finance companies the worst source of loans.

But Kenosha does not fit the expected pattern, falling instead between Madison and Racine in both ratings. The same is true for actual behavior of the debtors: Fewer Green Bay debtors reported finance companies as their biggest source of loans; the highest proportion using finance companies was in Racine. On another behavioral indicator, more Madison debtors showed an inclination to approve borrowing for a wider range of items than Racine, Kenosha, or Green Bay debtors. The ordering of the cities followed our expectation closely though not exactly: Madison, Racine, Kenosha, Green Bay. Finally, a related indicator showed Green Bay debtors to be more aware of interest rates on their loans than Madison, Kenosha, and Racine debtors—traditional norms of consumer behavior emphasize cost rather than immediacy of purchase. These data support Alford and Scoble's characterization of Green Bay and Kenosha as traditional and Madison and Racine as modern. The patterns distinguishing the public decision-making styles of these cities apparently spill over to private use of judicial agencies by both creditors and debtors.

Traditionalism also affects the legal culture. Only in Green Bay did most of the attorneys handling garnishment cases send out letters to the debtors prior to initiating the court action despite the cases having been extensively worked over by the creditor's collection department or a collection agency. Attorneys in Green Bay were more concerned about avoiding formal court action than attorneys in the other three cities, who reported that they immediately filed for court action unless they knew there had not been an active effort to collect.

Everything cannot be explained by cultural differences between the communities. The higher incidence of Chapter 13 proceedings as compared to bankruptcies in some of the cities is due to different evaluations of Chapter 13 by attorneys and to pressure exerted by the referees in bankruptcy. Where Chapter 13 proceedings are most frequent (in Madison and Racine)·, debtors report that lawyers often give them a real choice between it and bankruptcy. In Kenosha and Green Bay, lawyers rarely talk about Chapter 13 to bankruptcy clients and since these clients rarely heard of Chapter 13 from other sources, fewer used it.

Differences in attorney behavior are largely accounted for by the pressures they feel from the referee in bankruptcy and their relation to the Chapter 13 trustee, who handles the debtors affairs while he is under the plan. In Madison, the lawyer's preference for Chapter 13 proceedings can be traced to active campaigning in favor of it by the Madison Referee in Bankruptcy. Racine's higher Chapter 13 rate reflects the fact that the trustee was a fellow

Racine attorney, readily available on the telephone for consultation. Kenosha attorneys who also had to use the Racine trustee felt that Chapter 13 cases were beyond their control. They hesitated to incur the slight charge for a call to neighboring Racine. They preferred amortization under state law (although it provided less protection for the debtor) because they could maintain control over the proceedings and keep in close contact with the debtor who might later bring them higher fees in an accident or divorce case. Green Bay and Madison attorneys almost never used Wisconsin's amortization proceeding and did not speak of it as a lure to attract clients in better paying cases.

With only four cities, it is statistically impossible to estimate how much of the variation is explained by the political culture, by the legal culture, and by what appear to be accidental variations. Nevertheless, the wide variations discovered among four cities are significant.

This exploration of court usage in wage garnishment and consumer bankruptcy actions shows none of the usual political links between governmental action and private demands. To look for partisan biases of the judges (or referees), for evidence of other attitudinal biases in their decisions, for the linkage between the judicial selection process and court decisions, for the role of other political activities in this process, we would come away convinced that wage garnishment and bankruptcy are totally nonpolitical processes. Only an examination of patronage shows political processes at work, since the referees may appoint at will Chapter 13 trustees and trustees for all bankrupt estates. But Chapter 13 cases don't generate a great deal of revenue for the trustees and most straight bankruptcies by consumers involve either no or very limited assets so that the trustees benefit little from the cases. In the usual *partisan* sense, the processes examined are indeed nonpolitical.

Nevertheless, the courts are very political. Garnishment and bankruptcy cases invoke government power for private ends. Garnishment redistributes millions of dollars each year from the wages of debtors to the accounts of creditors. Bankruptcy results in the cancellation of other millions of dollars of indebtedness. The use of these court procedures also involves frequent harassment and considerable stigmatization. Although garnishment and bankruptcy are considered "private" proceedings, they significantly affect the distribution of material and symbolic values by government in the United States.

Thus it is politically significant that only a few of all eligible creditors and debtors use garnishment and bankruptcy proceedings. It means that government power is used to buoy what many consider to be the socially least desirable form of consumer credit—that extended by finance companies. The experience of wage earners with garnishment is likely to undermine their confidence in the courts as institutions which treat them justly and fairly. On the other hand, the use of bankruptcy by the minority of those eligible for it limits its benefits to the small group which happens to be well integrated into the legal system. Translating these findings to larger cities, it seems likely that in ghetto areas garnishment has even more disadvantageous effects in supporting undesirable credit and bankruptcy is even less used by the masses of alienated consumers who crowd the inner core.

The political process described is quite different from the electoral or legislative political processes political scientists ordinarily study. Instead, it resembles the administrative process which is becoming increasingly significant. The use of agricultural extension services, the use of counseling and educational services by the poor, the use of higher-education facilities by the young raise problems similar to those of court usage. None of these, however, involve, as wage garnishment and bankruptcy do, the dramatic use of the government coercive power for private objectives.

Government power can be invoked through far more routine ways than campaigning in elections. The consumption of government services is based on far different objectives than the ordinary use of government power through partisan means. Court actions, as well as other administrative decisions, frequently affect the core of people's personal behavior, their life-style, or fortune. They can color people's perception of the government and generate support for or alienation from it. We need to know what individuals and groups use such services and how they use them.

May 1969

FURTHER READING SUGGESTED BY THE AUTHOR:
Buy Now, Pay Later by Hillel Black (New York: Pocket Books, 1961) is an expose of credit schemes.
The Poor Pay More by David Caplovitz (New York: Macmillan-Free Press, 1963) describes the credit problems of impecunious consumers.

Lawyers for the Poor

DALLIN H. OAKS/WARREN LEHMAN

The Sixth Amendment to the Constitution requires that criminal defendants have access to a lawyer. That creates the problem of just how a lawyer should be obtained for the defendant who cannot afford to hire his own. Should the government pay private lawyers for taking on the criminal defense of the poor, or should it set up a bureau of full-time public defenders? If you take at face value the doctrine—necessary to the sound administration of the law—that all lawyers are equal, it. would seem the only way to decide this issue is on the basis of efficiency and economy.

Illinois is a good state in which to test this hypothesis. Illinois has a so-called mixed system: There is a public defender available to all indigents charged with crime, but in some circumstances a defendant may have a private counsel appointed to him instead of the defender. It is possible, therefore, to see the two systems in operation before the same judges and juries and under the same laws.

The data for our comparative study are all of the felony cases in Cook County for the year 1964. In talking about these cases we refer to 5,579 indictments; actually this is a synthetic figure, properly called "defendants by indictment," for a defendant may be named in more than one indictment and one indictment may name two or more defendants. The 5,579 indictments represent 4,040 defendants.

For our comparison, we divided defense counsel into three groups. About 40 percent of all indictments (2,226) were of indigents served by the Cook County public defender's office. About 4 percent (213) were of indigents defended by members of the Chicago Bar Association's Defense of Prisoners Committee. Though the committee's members handled only about half of the appointed-counsel cases, its records provide the only evidence of the work of appointed counsel. The remainder of the indictments (56 percent or 3,140) were defended by other private attorneys and largely represent the quality and style of service given defendants who manage to employ their own counsel. Of this group 95 percent were hired and paid by their clients. The others were appointed and paid by the state but cannot be separated statistically.

Before examining the data, something should be said of the general characteristics of these three groups.

The Cook County public defender's office is one of the oldest and largest in the country. It was founded in 1930 after the Defense of Prisoners Committee had spent five years studying the problems of indigent defense. In 1964 the defender's staff consisted of 21 assistants. (In 1966 it had 28.) Eleven of these had principal responsibility for the 2,226 felony indictments disposed in 1964, or about 200 cases a year for each man—far more than any attorney in private criminal practice. Many assistant defenders are young. They often go on the staff right out of law school just for this rapid introduction to criminal trial practice. A graduate entering the service gets $7,200 per year, probably a little less than his fellow who goes to work for a general practice private law firm in Chicago. For the person interested in criminal law, it's a good way to start.

Criminal law practice is a very chancy business. There are few private attorneys making good livings from the private practice of criminal law. Not many criminals have the money to pay a lawyer well. And you can't just hang your shingle out, say "Practice limited to criminal law," and expect the Mafia to beat a path to your door. The ranks of private lawyers doing criminal work include the few top men in the city, baffled family lawyers whose clients have fallen into the hands of the police, hacks who find their clients in the halls of the Criminal Courts building, corporation lawyers whose clients ask them to perform the work as a service, and young men on the way up who mix criminal and civil practice in the effort to make their way in the law without the benefit of a firm to feed, train, and provide them clients. Private retained lawyers are, therefore, a heterogeneous group, working on retainer, bringing to their clients both the best and the worst in ability and experience.

The members of the Defense of Prisoners Committee are quite likely to be associates of downtown law firms who for reason of principle or for the excitement of trial work make themselves available through the committee for court appointments to defend indigents. Each younger attorney is paired in a team with a senior attorney. There are about 50 such teams, which during 1964 handled between them about the same number of cases as a single public defender. The members of this committee are entitled, as is any attorney appointed to defend an indigent charged with a felony, to a fee up to $150 paid by the county, or $250 if the charge carries a possible death sentence. Many of the members don't collect their fees.

The statutory fees hardly compensate a lawyer who takes the time from a lucrative private practice to handle a lengthy criminal trial. On the other hand, the pay is not bad for the lawyer who merely pleads his client guilty or who hasn't much else in the way of practice. There are at least a few lawyers who earn a significant part of their income in statutory fees for appointments to defend indigents. In 1964 one attorney collected fees for appointments in 20 capital cases and 4 other felonies. Another collected in 5 capital cases and 18 other felonies. That's 47 fees between them. By comparison, the 100 or so members of the Defense of Prisoners Committee collected 118 fees. Committee members also had fewer capital case appointments (23) than the two specialists in appointment (who had 25 between them). Because of the lack of data, these appointed private counsel had to be lumped together for this study with the heterogeneous group of private retained counsel.

We have found significant differences in the style of operation favored by each of these groups as well as differences in where they have both their success and their failures. Overall, the differences suggest less that one kind of counsel is better than another than that they perform somewhat different roles in the overall operation of the criminal justice system.

The cause of these differences is another question. Differing ability—the most obvious inference—is only one possibility and not necessarily the most likely. Many factors, the relative weight of which we could not ascertain, influence trial success. Public defenders, for instance, have much less control over their clients. A private lawyer can threaten to walk away from the case when his advice is not followed; the defender cannot. The types of crimes may not be equally distributed among the three groups. And we know that, in general, the chance a person will be convicted varies radically according to the crime he is charged with. (This happens both because some types of crimes—forgery, for example—are likely to come with better evidence and because for some crimes—such as drunkenness—there is little enthusiasm for enforcement.) For every Speck case, the public defender gets thousands of impoverished defendants who have committed unspectacular crimes without imagination or style.

The differences associated with who one's lawyer is appear even before trial. Cases can be dismissed before trial for a number of reasons—because a defendant out on bond fails to show up for trial (the indictment is reinstated when he's caught), because a prosecutor having obtained a conviction on one count decided to drop another, because a defendant has died. If these were the only causes, a difference in pretrial dismissal rates would not be important. However, it is possible for a lawyer to have a pretrial hearing to decide such a question as whether evidence was improperly obtained. A defense lawyer can win a case by a successful motion to suppress evidence crucial to the prosecutor's case. Successful suppression before trial is likely to lead to a dismissal.

Our figures indicate that public defenders and bar association committee members get dismissals in about the same proportion of cases—8 percent for the defender and 6 percent for the committee member. In contrast, private retained counsel get dismissals in 29 percent of their cases.

The significance of this difference is almost impossible to assess. Unfortunately, the tags that are put upon various types of dismissal don't correspond to the reasons for dismissal that would interest us most. One tag, SOL (stricken with leave to reinstate) is used both for bail jumpers and for at least some evidentiary dismissals. Another, nolle prosequi, is used for evidentiary dismissals, too, as well as for dismissals when the prosecutor wins another case against the same defendant.

One thing we do know is that something like 300 defendants jumped bail. The majority of these had to be clients of retained counsel simply because the public defender and bar association counsel got only 100 SOL's between them—retained counsel got 577. But it is probably also true that bail jumpers are disproportionately represented among the clients of retained attorneys. It is, after all, those who can afford to pay lawyers who are more likely also to be able to post bond and get out on bail. Even discounting bail jumpers, there appears some residual advantage at this stage for retained counsel; we cannot similarly discount the retained counsel's more favorable rate of nolle prosequis.

With pretrial dismissals discounted, there remained 4,469 indictments to be disposed either on guilty plea or by trial. The decision whether to plead guilty or go to trial is first of all a tactical one, almost an exercise in gamesmanship. There are, as we noted, differences in the odds of conviction at trial depending on what crime is charged. The odds favoring success at trial must be weighed against the likelihood that a stiffer sentence will be imposed on the defendant who is convicted at trial. It is the favored treatment given those who plead guilty that keeps the number of trials within reasonable bounds. From the defendant's point of view the problem is one of weighing the certainty of a lesser penalty against the possibility of a stiffer one. Lawyers (and experienced defendants) are very sensitive to this problem, and nationally there is a very close correlation between guilty plea rates and the likelihood of conviction for the crime charged.

On guilty plea rate there is also a large discrepancy, though in this case the appointed counsel look more like private retained counsel and less like the public defender: 82 percent of the defender's clients plead guilty; the rate for private counsel is 68 percent and for appointed counsel 69 percent.

TABLE I—OVERALL DISPOSITIONS

	Public defender	Bar Association committee	Private and other appointed counsel
Dismissals before trial	8.0%	6.0%	29.0%
Found not guilty	8.2	11.0	5.8
Found guilty	8.4	18.0	12.2
Guilty pleas	75.4	63.1	53.0

Our finding compares closely with that of Lee Silverstein who in *Defense of the Poor* reported for Chicago in 1962 a 15 percent difference in plea rate between clients of the defender and those with retained counsel. The similarity we discovered between plea rates of retained and appointed counsel, however, runs contrary to the experience in federal courts in Chicago. The *Report of the Attorney General's Committee on Poverty and the Administration of Justice* issued in 1963 indicated that clients of appointed counsel plead guilty far more often than those with retained counsel. At the time of the study there was no public defender system in federal court. The difference may well have resulted from appointed counsel getting all of the problem clients that are absorbed in the state courts by the public defender. The attorney general's committee suggested that appointed counsel may advise a plea when the defendant lacks resources for an adequate defense. Whatever the merits of that suggestion with federal defendants, we found no evidence that bar association lawyers had such an attitude about their state defendants.

While it is true that either work pressure or the desire to please the judge with whom one works every day may influence an assistant public defender to encourage guilty pleas where a counsel under less pressure would advise a trial, trial is not always in the interest of a defendant. He will, after all, be less severely treated if he pleads guilty. There are probably extraneous pressures on both appointed and retained counsel to go to trial where in the abstract an attorney might advise a plea. Some lawyers have suggested that the retained counsel, having taken a fee, may feel he is bound to "go to the mat" to show that he has earned it. And trial work is exciting. While we have no evidence, it is reasonable to suppose that the volunteer defender from the bar committee may have some bias for the satisfaction to be gained from trial work.

There are other factors that may be operating to vary the plea rate. Second offenders and others who have been exposed to jail talk while awaiting trial may be more knowledgeable about the advantages of pleading guilty. If the public defender has a higher proportion of such clients —as he believes—this would tend to increase the number of clients who are willing to plead. And once again the discrepancy might be influenced by differences in the distribution of crimes charged.

Finally, the discrepancy could result from an advantage to the defender in bargaining with the prosecution over the type and length of sentence. One experienced prosecutor advised us that assistant state's attorneys can make a more favorable recommendation for the clients of the public defender than they could for retained counsel. The supervisor in the state's attorney's office may question their motivation if they seem unduly lenient with retained counsel, especially prominent counsel; the same doubts don't arise when the beneficiaries of bargaining are the assistant public defender and his indigent client. This theory is supported by the fact that about one-fifth of the defender's pleas are on reduced charges and that he seems to be somewhat more successful in getting probation for his clients.

By weeding out more of his clients with guilty pleas, the public defender improves his chance for success, compared to private and appointed counsel, on the 18 percent of his indictments he actually takes to trial. In 1964 he won acquittals in 50 percent of his trials. Committee counsel, who tried 32 percent of their cases, earned a 38 percent acquittal rate. Retained counsel have the worst record—23 percent acquittals on the 31 percent of their cases that go to trial.

If you combine guilty plea and conviction rates, thus including all cases decided on the merits, committee counsel come out best with an acquittal rate of 12 percent; the public defender wins acquittal for 9 percent; retained counsel win for only 7 percent. The relative success rate changes once again if we include pretrial dismissals. On that basis, retained counsel look best with 36 percent of all indictments ending either in dismissal or a finding of not guilty. The corresponding rate for committee counsel is 18 percent and for the public defender, 17 percent. A good part of the apparent advantage of the retained counsel disappears, of course, when we discount those dismissals that are due to clients jumping bail. Still it would appear that in at least some cases faulty evidence means release before trial for clients who have retained lawyers and victory in trial for indigent clients. This difference, too, may contribute to the relatively poor trial record of the retained attorneys.

Overall acquittal statistics hide some other important differences in the behavior of different types of counsel. A counsel who decides to go to trial may choose to try the case before either a judge or a jury. There is a difference between counsel in relative preference for a jury trial. Committee counsel go before a jury in about two-thirds of their trials, retained counsel do so in one-third; the public defender goes before a jury in only 15 percent of his cases. One possible contributing factor is that committee counsel may choose a jury trial to gain experience. The public defender, on the other hand, is very busy and very conscious of the probable extra penalty accruing to a defendant who loses his case before a jury. Just as there is a penalty for going to trial rather than pleading guilty, there is also a penalty for choosing the more expensive and time-consuming jury trial rather than a bench trial. In one case the trial judge stated on the record that he would have sentenced the defendant to one year to life in the penitentiary, but because the defendant had put the state to "the trouble of calling a jury" and had falsely protested his innocence in testimony, "it will cost you nine years additional, because the sentence is now 10 to life in the penitentiary." The sentence was reduced by the Illinois Supreme Court. Few judges are so naive as to allow such statements to appear in the record, but that philosophy—if not in such exaggerated a form—undoubtedly influences sentencing by most judges. Were that not so, every defendant would demand jury trial.

The assistant public defender who is permanently assigned to a single courtroom may be more aware of any hostility his judge has to jury trial. And since he has a backlog of other cases before the same judge, he may be

TABLE II—SUCCESS IN BENCH AND JURY TRIALS BY TYPE OF COUNSEL

	Public defender	Bar Association committee	Private and other appointed counsel	All counsel
Bench trials: Acquitted	55%	48%	20%	34%
Convicted	45%*	52	80	66
Number of Defendants	312	23	476	811
Jury trials: Acquitted	18%	33%**	30%	28%
Convicted	82	67	70	72
Number of Defendants	55	40	231	326

* Includes 3% found guilty of a lesser charge.
** Includes 10% that terminated in a "hung" jury.

more sensitive to the overall delay caused by demanding a jury.

Finally, the defender may hesitate to demand a jury trial because he is far more successful in bench trials. The defender in 1964 won 55 percent of his bench trials but only 18 percent of his jury trials. Committee counsel, by comparison, won 48 percent of their bench trials and 33 percent of their jury trials. The discrepancy in success rates is, therefore, not so great. Retained counsel are the only ones who do better before juries than before judges. They got only 20 percent acquittals in bench trials, but got 30 percent before juries—not quite as good a rate before juries as the bar association counsel. (It is only fair to add that the defender has won as many as 46 percent of his jury trials—in 1965—and that the figure varies greatly from year to year. Unfortunately, statistics for other types of counsel in other years are not available.)

Despite all these differences in what happens to defendants with each type of lawyer, there is a surprising similarity in the total of all clients, whatever type of counsel they have, who are convicted by plea or trial. Committee counsel have a conviction rate of 88 percent, the public defender 91 percent, and retained counsel 93 percent. One might say that the type of counsel makes little difference in whether or not one is found guilty. However, it is often a trap to assume that similar results are produced by similar causes.

We have reached the final point in the criminal process, the sentencing. Because there is no information on the comparative length of prison sentences or frequency of death sentences, the only comparison that can be made is with respect to how often a convicted felon is put on probation rather than given a jail sentence. We found that in 1964 the public defender obtained probation for 28 percent of his clients, compared with 14 percent for all other counsel. However, in a sample of 163 cases made two years earlier, Silverstein found that the public defender had a probation rate of only 18 percent compared with a 39 percent rate for retained counsel. Our result, based on a much larger sample, compares more closely to expectation. If a guilty plea can increase the chances for probation or lead to a lighter sentence, as is generally believed, then the public defender's style of representation should offer the best prospect for the average defendant. If the case is one which ought to be tried by a jury, retained or committee counsel would be better.

What we have shown is that the various types of counsel have rather different styles of defense and that these styles may be more or less appropriate for different defendants, depending upon their positions. Those against whom the evidence and law are clear would be ill served by the lawyer whose insistence on a full-fledged trial results in a stiffer penalty. The defendant trapped in a web of circumstantial evidence will want the full attention of the most able and unharried trial lawyer. So too will the one who believes a jury will never convict him.

It seems to us advisable to maintain parallel systems simply to provide diversity in style of representation, to provide the indigent a range of choice. But that is not the only reason. While there is no question of either the integrity or ability of assistant public defenders, it may be that the quality of public defense is maintained by the opportunity of the accused to reject the defender and demand a private lawyer. The private appointed lawyer can set a very high standard of indigent defense, operating without the pressures of volume that continually impinge on the defender. And they can and do take causes, devoting amounts of time, energy, and money that could not be asked of a public servant.

Finally, the appointed counsel have a special function as a result of their interest and ability in jury trials. In their study *The American Jury* Hans Zeisel and Harry Kalven Jr. suggest that the jury trial sets standards both for the bench and the opposing attorneys. They state that decisions to waive a jury trial or to plead guilty "are in part informed by expectations of what the jury will do. Thus, the jury is not only controlling the immediate case before it, but the host of cases not before it which are destined to be disposed of in the pretrial process." Through the jury the public gets a chance to express its views of criminal law enforcement. The indigents whose cases are deserving of consideration by this court of last resort are as entitled to its review as are those who can employ counsel.

We regret, therefore, any tendency—even in the name of economy—to reduce the role of the private lawyer in indigent defense. The evidence of the defender's economy is doubtful at best, and the private lawyer's participation in a spirit of public service may well be the touchstone of continued integrity in the treatment of the poor.

July/August 1967

FURTHER READING SUGGESTED BY THE AUTHORS:

The American Jury by Harry J. Kalven, Jr., and Hans Zeisel (Boston: Little, Brown & Co., 1966). A study of the operation of the jury and judge as finders of fact in criminal cases.

Defense of the Poor in Criminal Cases by Lee Silverstein (American Bar Foundation, 1965). A national field study on methods of indigent defense and attitudes of judges and lawyers.

The Rationing of Justice by Harold S. Trebach (New Brunswick, N.J.:,Rutgers University Press, 1964). A general summary of the criminal process and indigent defense, written for the layman.

Advocacy in the Ghetto

RICHARD A. CLOWARD/RICHARD M. ELMAN

There are 500,000 people in New York City living on welfare payments, but until November 1965 no delegation of public dependents had been received in the office of a Commissioner of Welfare for more than 30 years. (The last time was in the days of the Worker's Alliance, a union of recipients and public welfare workers.) Three decades had gone by since welfare recipients had presented their needs and their grievances directly to the man in charge. This is the story of events that led up to that meeeting—a story of how social workers turned into advocates in order to secure their clients' rights from the welfare bureaucracy and of how recipients themselves began to organize for action. It suggests a pattern that can be used elsewhere in the country to deal with the daily problems of living under the welfare state.

In November 1962 a social worker from Mobilization for Youth and one assistant moved into an unoccupied storefront at 199 Stanton Street on New York's Lower East Side. It was located in an apartment building which did not then rent to Negroes, Puerto Ricans, or persons on welfare.

Across the street was a *bodega*. Another grocery, down the block, was the principal numbers racket drop for the area. MFY put some chairs and couches in the brightly painted waiting room in the front of the store. Then a sign was painted on the front windows: CENTRO DE SERVICO AL VECENDARIO . . . NEIGHBORHOOD SERVICE CENTER. On the door was lettered: WALK IN! Many Stanton Street residents, 14 percent of whom are on public assistance, accepted the invitation. They were invited to describe their problems. The MFY workers soon found that the lengthy verbal charge sheet made by people against the hostile environment in which they were forced to live, could be distilled into a grievance against "welfare."

It soon became clear to branch director Joseph Kreisler that unresolved problems with public welfare were a crucial factor in the instability of life along Stanton Street. If people didn't have enough welfare they weren't able to pay their bills at the grocer. If they didn't get their welfare checks on time, they would be in trouble with their landlords. If welfare didn't provide money for school clothing, they would have to keep their children home from school and would have difficulties with the authorities. This day-to-day relationship with the welfare bureaucracy was making people bitter and angry and punitive toward one another.

But, if the pattern seemed clear to Kreisler and his supervisor, Sherman Barr, those who complained most bitterly were not able to pinpoint the sources of their misery quite so precisely. As one man put it, "I feel that the City of New York has abandoned me." Others told of harrowing experiences with welfare officials as if such dealings were the way that things should be. Since they had never been led to expect any better treatment from such an agency, they had no awareness of their rights under the law.

It became necessary, therefore, for the MFY workers to assure people that they did have rights, and to demonstrate that their rights could be upheld and defended without recriminations. Such a determination by the workers often required a dogmatic conviction about injustice. One of them put it this way:

When I think that Mrs. Cortez hasn't gotten any money for her rat allowance I sometimes want to throw up my hands and say: What difference does it make? Why should people in this day and age have rat allowances? (A New York City welfare policy allows slum families extra allowances toward their utility bills to offset the cost of keeping their lights burning all night as a deterrence against rats.) But when I realize that it isn't just the rat allowance . . . that it's a total system of oppressiveness and disrespect for people, why then I've got to get her that rat allowance. I've got to help her get as many things as possible.

Few of the workers were at first so dogmatic. Kreisler, for example, was a veteran of the public welfare systems of New York and Maine, familiar with the savagery of some welfare policies and the Pecksniffian quality of others (such as a New York City regulation which makes it mandatory to mail clients' checks out late before a weekend so that they will not have the money to spend on drink). But even he had his "eyes opened" by the volume of abuses that were recorded by workers through the testimony of their clients.

In its first six months of operation, 199 Stanton Street received more than 200 families from an immediate three or-four block radius who attested to their antagonistic relationship with the Department of Welfare. Through the neighborhood grapevine many soon learned to come directly to Stanton Street after an affront at one of the local welfare centers. In addition, of the non-welfare families who came during those first six months, nearly two-thirds listed "insufficient income" as their principal problem, which meant, in many cases, that they were not getting welfare benefits even though they were eligible. At 199 Stanton Street the social workers discovered that the problems of their clients were so tied to the bureaucratic workings of the city that they could keep their storefront open profitably only from 9 to 5 on weekdays, the normal working hours of public agencies.

This came as a distinct surprise to supervisory personnel at MFY. They had originally hoped to bring their workers more intimately in touch with the day-to-day affairs of their clients departing from traditional psycho-therapeutic methods and offering instead specific and practical advice on problems of health, housing, welfare, education, and employment. But even here, they saw their chief function as liaisons between clients and agencies; they did not yet realize that even these concrete activities would fail to resolve issues between the poor and the welfare state. Many workers soon found, however, that they had to do something more than refer, advise, and counsel if they were to get results. They were being called upon to take sides in a pervasive dispute between their clients and an agency of the welfare state. When they refused to do so, their clients abandoned them. A new practice soon evolved which came to be known as *advocacy*.

An advocate in this context is one who intervenes between an agency of government and his client to secure an entitlement or right which has thus far been obscured or denied. To act effectively, the advocate must have sufficient knowledge of the law and of the public agency's administrative procedures to recognize injustice when it occurs and then seek a solution in harmony with his client's interests. In practice, the Stanton Street advocates often found that they had to instruct the representatives of welfare agencies in the law and how it should be interpreted. One of the advocate's most demanding tasks was to serve notice on his opposite number within the welfare bureaucracy that he was prepared to move a notch further up the hierarchy if justice was not tendered on the present level.

Thus the advocates listened to endless tales of woe. They counted up scores of welfare budgets to detect possible underbudgeting. They placed telephone calls to a great number of functionaries and sometimes accompanied clients when they went to see these people in person. They argued and they cajoled. They framed rebuttals to cases put forward by welfare, but they also charged negligence.

They attacked as well as defended. When, for example, a Stanton Street woman was charged with child neglect, the alert worker was able to show that she had been consistently under-budgeted for more than a year, making her efforts at successful child-rearing virtually impossible. When another client was evicted for non-payment of rent, the worker attempted to force welfare to make the payment —because he could show that it had failed repeatedly in its legal obligation to do so.

But, whether their threats were applied with politeness or out of anger, out of careful manipulation or a blustering disregard for the sensibilities of their opposite numbers, the primary force of such advocacy was in serving notice upon the low-level employee that he would be held responsible for his actions to his supervisor and on up the line. Thus advocacy was the bludgeon by which this city agency was made responsive to a portion of its Lower East Side constituency. At 199 Stanton Street the workers came to serve as surrogates for their clients with the bureaucratically arranged world outside the welfare ghetto.

This often militant advocacy was always carried on with a calculated informality. Young people were not discouraged from idling about the place, any client was free to come and go as he pleased; parties were held on holidays; neighborhood people were employed as janitors, clericals, and translators. Many of the professional workers and "case-aides" were either Negro or Puerto Rican, and there was little attention given to any differentiation of duties according to professional status. Moreover, the center managed to keep up an active and informative interviewing referral practice when clients came in with requests for other kinds of service. When a client came for help with welfare it was always possible for him to receive a loan or even a small outright gift of cash to tide him over while his case was being adjudicated. An effort was also made to keep a supply of clean used clothing on hand for those whose requests from welfare might take more than a few hours to resolve.

However, even though as much as $600 was given out in some months in small grants, the major reason that people were drawn to the center was that the workers took sides. They were willing to put themselves out to uphold their clients' rights under the welfare state. One Puerto Rican mother put it this way: "When you go alone to welfare they treat you like dirt. When you go with a social worker it's different."

After a year it became clear to the administration of MFY that the indignation of the social worker was not sufficient protection against the injustices of the social welfare state. So the agency established a free legal service to take referrals from neighborhood centers such as the storefront on Stanton Street. These attorneys applied themselves to eviction proceedings in public and private housing; they dealt with consumer frauds and other specialized areas of practice among the poor. But they also began to challenge decisions concerning welfare clients where the facts were at issue, or where actions had been taken in seeming violation of the intent of the law.

As a case in point, one might cite the New York State Welfare Abuses Act, passed in 1962 as a compromise measure to satisfy demands that New York bar public assistance to applicants from out of state. It was clearly stipulated by the legislators that only persons who could be shown to have come to New York for the express purpose of collecting relief could be lawfully denied such a benefit. In actual practice, however, the new resident's mere appearance at a welfare center to apply for relief was often taken as sufficient justification to deny him benefits.

By 1964 four attorneys were employed full time at MFY on cases brought to their attention by the social workers. It was because these lawyers threatened litigation that the local Department of Welfare center no longer invoked the Welfare Abuses Act as a matter of course. It was fear of litigation which prompted the department to abandon its policy of after-midnight intrusions on the residences of AFDC mothers to detect the presence of males—a policy which seemed a clear-cut violation of the normal guarantees of privacy. The workers at Stanton Street were encouraged to bring those cases to the attention of MFY attorneys through which the legality of administrative acts could be contested in open hearings, so that precedents could be established.

Nevertheless, the lawyers also spent a good deal of their time advising workers and clients about how to adopt lawful and proper strategies to exploit those rights which did seem vested. Working closely with the social workers, the lawyers contested capricious eligibility rulings and attempted to reinstate eligibles whose benefits had been arbitrarily terminated. At times they argued the merits of the case. At other times they argued that the law had been perverted by bad administrative policies. The lawyers were prepared to represent the clients at the formal appeals tribunals of the state Department of Social Welfare, but they found that a majority of client grievances did not need to come before such "fair hearings." Often, just a telephone call from an MFY attorney expressing interest in a particular case served to persuade a functionary that he was acting without respect to a person's rights.

Because of welfare's desire to avoid establishing precedents and hence to settle out of court, the MFY legal service was able to litigate only a small percentage of the cases it was called in on, but its impact upon the legal vacuum within the welfare ghetto was impressive. Even after the addition of this free legal service, the workers at Stanton Street continued to be confronted with the bulk of cases requiring immediate advocacy; but they could now defend their clients' rights reinforced by the legal expertise of Edward Sparer (the first MFY legal director) and his associates. Moreover, they were able to increase their sophistication about welfare law through their continuing association with the attorneys, and they passed on some of this education to their opposite numbers in the welfare bureaucracy.

Even the clients benefited educationally from the program. Many had never before had any contacts with attorneys, except, perhaps, as their adversaries. Now these attorneys were representing them in adversary proceedings against the Department of Welfare, and they became aware of the power which proper representation bestows upon the private citizen. As one AFDC mother stated: "I trust the lawyers more than anybody because they would make a living if there were no poor people." When a bitter and prolonged strike afflicted the Department of Welfare in the winter of 1964-65, some MFY workers and clients from Stanton Street demonstrated in support of the welfare workers to signify that their complaints were against laws and policies, not individuals.

By the summer of 1963 MFY had established three other neighborhood centers along the Lower East Side. The agency's supervisory staff decided to solicit even more clients by publicizing its services through handbills, posters, and mass meetings. Some workers had also begun to seek out clients in distress, among other ways by reading newspaper accounts in the Spanish-language press. The strategy of the centers was now fixed. They were given a definite set of priorities for intervention with city agencies, of which welfare was to be the pre-eminent target.

This increasing attention to the advocacy tactic meant that the workers had to contend with increasing antagonism from the welfare department. The commissioner was angered, for example, by the threats of aggressive court action against welfare. The lower-echelon functionaries were angered by their harassment by MFY and would often respond with open hostility to calls from Stanton Street employees. "When I go to welfare," one Stanton Street worker declared, "I don't wait around for the stall. If I don't get treated with respect, I start hollering for the supervisor." Another said: "Any way you cut it they are the enemy." Perhaps this explains what one welfare worker meant when she described MFY's staff as "rude, angry, and non-professional." The accusation was also continually being made that some MFY workers lacked information about public-welfare policies in taking on their advocacy positions. But, since many Stanton Street workers were former welfare employees, it seems more reasonable to suppose that they were merely placing more liberal interpretations upon existing welfare regulations. Where, for example, some welfare caseworkers might use improvidence to justify not making an additional grant for a client, the Stanton Street workers would insist upon the person's legal right to such an entitlement beyond his supposed characteralogical defect.

One veteran employee with more than 30 years in the Department of Welfare was critical of the MFY policy of giving money to people on some occasions rather than forcing welfare to make these payments. However, though she found some of MFY's advocacy tactics "a little hard to bear," she was generally appreciative of the effects. "If we were doing our job," she said, "you wouldn't need any neighborhood centers . . . and if there were more neighborhood centers like this in the city of New York," she added, "we might have to begin to do a better job. . . . I learned what my workers were doing with some clients from the neighborhood service center. I might never have known otherwise." When this same person subsequently retired from the Department of Welfare, she was hired as a consultant by MFY to help cut through the knotty complex of rules and regulations by which people on Stanton Street were being governed. "What this proves to me," said one MFY staff member, "is that you have to work 30 years in the department to be able to get people what they are entitled to . . . and they expect our clients to just walk in and apply. . . ."

Such comments reflected the increasing hostility between welfare and the workers on Stanton Street. The workers also showed a tendency to exhibit hostility toward and impatience with their clients, who by now had transferred some of their previous dependency on welfare to the storefront on Stanton Street. "Can't these people do anything themselves?" was a phrase frequently heard among the workers.

Many of the workers seemed to be developing a resentment at having to perform rudimentary "non-professional" services on behalf of their clients over and over again, and some of the clients were also restless, spurred on, in part, by their activities in various MYF social-action programs. Presently the program heads, Barr and Kreisler, began to wonder whether, if the clients were given staff support and encouragement, they could begin to take over some of these practical efforts to deal with the welfare system. They reasoned, for example, that if 50 clients all needed the same items of clothing it might be more effective to make one request on behalf of 50 rather than 50 individual requests. They reasoned, too, that this strategy might coerce welfare into making certain of its grants more automatic, or, rather, less discretionary.

So, after three years, the center on Stanton Street decided to hire a "community organizer" to bring people together around their most commonly held interest—public welfare.

In the hot summer months Stanton Street people rarely go away on vacations. They start worrying about the cold months ahead. They know if they do not begin to bother their welfare workers about clothing for the winter, their requests may never be fulfilled. Thus, in the late summer of 1965, they came to make their usual requests to the advocate at 199 Stanton Street. Would the workers talk to welfare? Would they tell them what they needed? To their surprise they were advised to go next door and speak to the Committee of Welfare Families.

The Committee of Welfare Families was hardly more than a name at the time, although the concept of community action was certainly not novel to people on Stanton

Street. Many of the initial membership cadre had already participated in rent strikes and civil rights demonstrations, but, where these were activities of short duration, the committee hoped to be an ongoing organization. Aside from a few of the local women, who had been most active previously, there was an MFY attorney and social-work organizer, Ezra Birnbaum. Birnbaum went to great efforts to make the group appear to be like any other voluntary membership organization, but, in fact, the women continually referred to him as their "social worker"

When clients went to see Birnbaum and the neighborhood women who were working with him, they were told that the group would bring together Negroes and Puerto Ricans who had common problems with welfare. If they wanted to be part of the group, they were asked to make surveys of their winter clothing needs and then bring them to the committee, which would attempt to act as the bargaining agents for all of them. Within a month over 90 families had agreed to the procedure, and the first tentative strategies were proposed.

"We chose the winter clothing issue," Birnbaum has since pointed out, "because it was something that genuinely concerned people . . . because they had so many small children . . . and because the injustice was so blatant. Many people hadn't gotten coats in six or seven years. Here was an issue we could exploit which would genuinely benefit our people. . . ."

The winter clothing issue also went to the heart of the perennially nagging question of what constituted a welfare entitlement. Every welfare family is budgeted a very small sum semi-monthly with which to augment clothing supplies. Invariably this sum is used for ordinary living expenses because grants for food are so low. In addition, it was department policy to allow special grants of approximately

$150 a year per family for winter clothing, but these grants were usually not given out unless requested, and, even then, the family usually got less than the full amount. In October 1965, individual workers at all the welfare centers serving residents of the MFY area began to receive neat, concise letters from their clients. It was clear that they had all been prepared by one agency and mailed out simultaneously, but, since they were written as individual requests, it was not immediately clear to welfare what was behind this sudden flurry of letters which read:

I would like to request winter clothing for my children and myself. I would appreciate it if you would grant this request as quickly as possible, as the weather is cold at this time. My family is in need of the following items of winter clothing. . . .

There followed individual itemized requests for coats, children's snowsuits, coveralls, boots, scarves, woolen skirts. All these requests had been certified by the committee as being in accord with current welfare schedules. When, after a few weeks, the welfare caseworkers did not reply, a follow-up letter was sent, with copies to supervisory personnel at welfare. When this effort also netted scant results, the committee as a group wrote to Commissioner Louch-heim:

We, as members of the Committee of Welfare Families of the Lower East Side, have written letters to our investigators requesting winter clothing. . . . The first 21 letters were mailed between October 12th and October 15th. Of these, only 9 have received any money at all, and none of these nine have been given enough money to keep their families warm this winter. *More important, the other 12 families have received no money at all!*

We feel that we are being neglected—especially since many of our investigators haven't even been in touch with us to find out about the seriousness of the situation.

Winter is here; our children are cold. Many of us are unable to keep clinic appointments because we do not have proper clothing. Many of our children have caught colds which can lead to other serious illnesses. Some of our children haven't been to school since the weather turned cold.

In most years, many of us have had to wait until December, January, or even later to buy our winter clothing. This year, we're not willing to wait that long and see our children have to wear thin summer clothing when it gets below freezing. That is why we asked Mobilization for Youth to help us this year.

Commissioner Louchheim—we feel we have waited long enough to receive our winter clothing. . . . We need your help in securing winter clothing for all our members before the weather gets any colder.

We request that our meeting with you be held within the next 3 days.

The committee waited three days. When the commissioner did not respond to their letter, they were prepared to picket at his office but were prevailed upon by MFY to send a telegram instead:

You received letter from us on Monday November 15 requesting meeting with you to discuss our members needs for winter clothing. We received no reply. Our children are cold. Winter is here. Our investigators have not answered our letters or have not given us enough money to keep children warm. We need your help before weather gets colder. We will be at your office to meet with you Tuesday November 23 1:30 p.m.

That same day the commissioner replied by telegram (after attempting to telephone) that he would be able to meet with the committee on Friday, November 26, at 1:30 p.m. In the meantime he would endeavor to get information on each of the cases specified in the documents attached to the committee's original ultimatum.

The meeting which took place between the welfare commissioner and the Committee of Welfare Families was, in the commissioner's own words, the first such meeting between a commissioner and a New York City client group in over 30 years. All of the welfare recipients had been well briefed by Birnbaum on what they would say to the commissioner, but, in fact, protest proved to be unnecessary. The commissioner quickly agreed that all members of the committee who were entitled to winter clothing would receive it, and he further formalized the bargaining status of the committee of Lower East Side families by outlining a formal grievance procedure. Clients were to continue to make their requests either by mail or in person through their workers at the various welfare centers. He would thenceforth instruct all workers to acknowledge the receipt of these requests immediately and in writing. If, within 10 days, no reply was received to an individual client's request, the committee was free to contact predesignated liaison personnel at each of the welfare centers serving the neighborhood, who would be empowered to act so that their grievances could be corrected.

The hard-pressed membership of the Committee of Welfare Families was quick to interpret their meeting with the commissioner as a victory. By agreeing to consult with them as a group about their needs, he had implicitly recognized for perhaps the first time in their careers as welfare clients that they had a legitimate corporate interest in helping to determine the rules of their own dependency. In the days that followed many of these families began to receive generous checks from the Department of Welfare to purchase winter clothing.

There were further meetings arranged with the designated liaison personnel at the various welfare centers to arrange bargaining procedures. The women were delighted that they could dictate just who and how many of their number could be in attendance at these formal procedures. Thus, when the department tried to insist that only members of the committee could meet with welfare officials, the women held firm in their insistence that the committee could designate anybody it chose to represent it at these meetings, and the Department of Welfare was forced to give in on this point. And, as most of the Lower East Side families began to have their winter clothing needs satisfied, the women decided to take up other issues such as budgeting. They requested that all members ask for budgets from their caseworkers if they did not already have them and, if they did have them, to bring them to the committee where they could be properly scrutinized.

The committee also began to elect officers. It designated sub-committees to investigate various new problem areas having to do with their welfare dependency. The leadership attended briefing sessions with MFY's attorneys in an effort to acquire a better understanding of their legal rights. Gradually, as the natural leadership potentials of some of the women emerged more clearly, MFY's paid organizer began to function more as an adviser than as a leader. One of the women gave this explanation for the process:

Some of us know we are going to be on welfare the rest of our lives. They know it and we know it. So it's about time to act like we know it. It's about time we started acting like human beings.

For the unemployed or under-employed men who have still not been organized, Stanton Street's workers have much work to do in beginning to provide them with the entitlements which they have thus far been denied. "It wouldn't be so bad living here," one of these men told us, "if you were rich. We're not rich. All we have is the welfare. That means freezing in the winter and boiling in the summer. It means living on credit when we can't afford it. It means lying. It means doing without. . . . When I come home in the evening my wife has been at Bellevue which is uptown and maybe at Church Street, all the way across town, and I'm wondering where she got the money for the carfare. . . . "

The storefront on Stanton Street has been in existence a little less than four years, and its work has increased tenfold, with two offices added. It is still too early to evaluate its permanent contributions to life in the community. Its powers have been limited. It has not yet been able to change substantially the terms of economic dependency when it still seems to be the consensus among most legislators and their constituents that such dependency is to be discouraged, abhored, and punished.

Many more people from Stanton Street are on welfare than before. The storefront's clients are better clothed, better housed, and better fed than they were four years ago. Many now have telephones, quite a few have washing machines and television sets.

Are they better people? Are they worse? Such questions seem like the supreme irrelevancy. For if they are not better for their improved economic circumstances, the society is better for their actions against it. Democracy cannot be said to exist where government is allowed to oppress its citizens so blatantly.

December 1966

Justice Stumbles over Science

DAVID L. BAZELON

Modern criminal law lives almost as much in the shadow of Freud as of Blackstone. For a generation now, law and other social institutions have been receiving revolutionary new information about human beings from the behavioral sciences. This information seldom solves our problems; in fact, it often seems to complicate them.

Some judges and lawyers say that the findings of behavioral science are too revolutionary to be allowed in the courtroom. But I cannot see that we have any choice but to allow them. To quote Havelock Ellis:

> . . . However imperfect the microscope may be, would it be better to dispense with the microscope? Much less when we are dealing with criminals, whether in the court of justice or in the prison, or in society generally, can we afford to dispense with such science of human nature as we may succeed in attaining.

Science does not create complexities for the law—it reveals them.

Are the two systems—law and science—properly informed about and related to each other? We have problems about introducing new knowledge and understanding into the legal system and problems about the differences between the philosophies of science and of law. But as a judge I am primarily troubled by the man in the dock—about how the behavioral sciences are used in our criminal courts.

Over 100 years ago English law produced the M'Naghten rule to be used in deciding whether an accused person should be excused on the ground of insanity. That rule has come to symbolize one of the great debates between law and the behavioral sciences. M'Naghten provided:

> The party accused must be labouring under such a defect of reason, from disease of the mind, as not to know the nature and quality of the act he was doing, or, if he did know it, that he did not know he was doing what was wrong.

The United States adopted England's M'Naghten rule. In our time it has evoked swelling criticism from psychiatrists who say it places undue emphasis on man's reason and fails to recognize the emotional forces that drive him. A judge on my court put it this way:

> Psychiatry does not conceive that there is a separate little man in the top of one's head called reason whose function it is to guide another unruly little man called instinct, emotion, or impulse in the way he should go. The tendency of psychiatry is to regard what ordinary men call reasoning as a rationalization of behavior rather than the real cause of behavior.

Yet only if a defendant suffers from a defect of reason—of cognition—can he be excused from criminal responsibility under M'Naghten's rule. M'Naghten treats the insanity defense as a hole in the dike of responsibility, to be kept as small as possible lest the dike be weakened.

A story will illustrate how harshly this rule still operates and how this harshness is rationalized. Seven years ago a young man aged 22, Don White, beat an old woman to death and a few hours later stabbed to death a dockworker whom he had never met before. In neither case did the defendant flee from the scene of the crime. He waited to chat with passers-by and to watch the police come and go.

The court was told about his background. Don White had never lived with his mother. She was only 13 when he was born. When he was four months old, she left him at a railway depot. A porter turned him over to the woman who became his adoptive mother. Despite his superior intelligence—his IQ was about 130—White was expelled from every school he attended. He was in state institutions nine times, with a growing record of violence and delinquency. In 1951 a child psychiatrist said he was suffering from "a very malignant mental illness," that "institutionalization is absolutely necessary," and that "he will almost certainly wind up in prison or in a state mental hospital."

Between his chance meeting in the depot with his adoptive mother and his murderous chance meeting with the dockworker 20 years later, White was the subject of social service and of psychiatric studies time and time again.

What happened when—as we piously say—"he had his day in court?" Despite evidence of serious mental disorder, the defense of insanity was rejected because it was said that he was intelligent—that is, he had a high IQ and knew right from wrong. He was sentenced to die. The appellate court refused to alter the M'Naghten test:

The question before us is whether we, as the majority of jurisdictions, should refuse to extend absolute immunity from criminal responsibility to persons who, although capable of understanding the nature and quality of their acts (the ability to distinguish between right and wrong), are unable to control their own behavior as a result of mental disease or defect. . . . One argument for such change is that we must take advantage of new developments in psychiatry. [But] there is nothing new about the idea that some people who know what they are doing still cannot control their actions.

Recognizing that no new knowledge was necessary to see that White was grossly disordered, the court held that the insanity defense "is available only to those persons who have lost contact with reality so completely that they are beyond any of the influences of the criminal law." The court decided to retain the M'Naghten rule since it "better serves the basic purpose of the criminal law—to minimize crime in society. . . . When M'Naghten is used, all who might possibly be deterred from the commission of criminal acts are included within the sanctions of the criminal law."

Another horrible, but not atypical, example of the operation of M'Naghten is the New York case of an 18-year-old college freshman who killed his father. This boy was termed a schizophrenic by the examining psychiatrists. The murder was done several days before the young man was to take his final examinations in college, and apparently one of his psychotic reasons for committing the act was to avoid taking them. His disordered mind had made some connection between escape from taking the examinations, for which he was unprepared, and his hatred of his father and desire to reside again with his mother. On cross-examination, the prosecuting attorney attacked the doctor's diagnosis with a rather traditional line of questioning:

Q. . . . First, Doctor, psychiatry is not an exact science, is it?

A. Well, that's a matter of opinion.

Q. Well, let's put it this way, Doctor. Is it generally considered to be an exact science in the same sense that internal medicine or surgery is an exact science?

The prosecutor included an effort to show that the doctor was expressing a mere opinion, that the defendant did not suffer from an "organic" disease, that the doctor's perception of symptoms was "subjective"—and in general that the diagnosis had been made by a psychiatrist rather than an IBM machine.

But most strikingly in this case, the prosecuting attorney pursued a line of questioning based apparently on the assumption that if the boy knew that the knife in his hand when he killed his father was a knife and not a toothbrush, that if when he tried to hitch a ride to his home town on the night of the murder he knew he was headed for Elmira, New York, and not Timbuktu, and so on, *then* he knew what he was doing. Here is an excerpt from the testimony:

Q. ... He knew then on the Thursday before the murder when he went down and procured a knife that he was procuring a knife, didn't he?

A. He knew he had a knife. But he had a delusional motive when it came to the killing.

Q. Doctor, if you please, will you kindly just answer my question. ...

May I have the last part stricken?
The Court. Strike it out.

Q. Doctor, he knew the purpose for which he secured the knife, did he not?

A. He had a psychotic motivation at that time.

The Court. Answer the question.

More of the same follows, page after page of the transcript. The jury found the defendant guilty of murder in the first degree, and the New York Court of Appeals upheld the ruling and affirmed the death penalty.

I am reminded of the nineteenth century English judge, Lord Bramwell, who quaintly expressed his approval of the M'Naghten rule in these terms:

I think that, although the present law lays down such a definition of madness, that nobody is hardly ever really mad enough to be within it, yet it is a logical and good definition.

During my first three years on the bench I became increasingly troubled while passing on and reading cases like the ones I have just recounted. Many lawyers, judges, and jurors were troubled. Psychiatrists were protesting the resistance to use of their new understandings. Even when they were allowed to testify freely in court, the M'Naghten rule was, in effect, an invitation to disregard most of their testimony.

On the simple premise that fact-finders should be able to weigh any and all expert information about the accused's behavior, I wrote an opinion for my court which held that the M'Naghten rule was no longer adequate. That opinion, in the 1954 case of *Durham v. United States,* held that an accused is not criminally responsible "if his act was the product of mental disease or defect." We pointed out that:

The science of psychiatry now recognizes that a man is an integrated personality and that reason, which is only one element in that personality, is not the sole determinant of behavior.

All we sought to do was to give those who are charged with assessing the responsibility of a mentally disordered offender the data which modern understanding requires. Yet Durham raised a controversy in legal and behavioral circles similar to the controversy aroused in wider circles by the Supreme Court's decision of the same year which rejected the old notion that separate treatment of Negroes could really be equal. Opposition to the integration decisions is fast abating. Not so with the Durham decision.

The Durham rule has been adopted in very few of our states. Yet it has been considered, I believe, by the highest court of every state and by most federal courts as well. With such widespread "rejection," why does Durham command so much attention and so much opposition? Why is the controversy it aroused still such a live issue? I suggest that Durham touched an exposed nerve in the administration of criminal justice. We are all troubled by punishing people who suffer from mental and emotional disorders.

There was some amelioration of M'Naghten even before Durham, such as the "irresistible impulse" rule. There has been more since. Nonetheless, there remains a persistent reluctance to include information about sick people. At one level, this could be simple resistance to change. But in all fairness, it seems more complicated. It is a special aspect of the stress which has risen as we have tried to build a better bridge between two systems: our legal system, with its reluctance to assimilate knowledge from the behavioral sciences; and the behavioral sciences themselves, with their reluctance to clarify the state of the developing body of knowledge about human nature.

Why are professionals on each side failing to adapt? Why does the law find it so difficult to assimilate information which behavioral science has to offer? The principal reason, I believe, is uncertainty about where this information might lead.

We are in that terrible period known as "meanwhile." The behavioral sciences tell us enough to reveal the gross imperfections of present solutions, but not enough to provide perfect alternatives. Furthermore, what we are told is not limited to those recognizably mentally ill. Some light is also shed on those whom the law and society had always thought "bad" rather than "sick." The distinguished British sociologist Barbara Wootton points to the implications:

> The creation of the new category of psychopaths is the thin end of what may eventually prove to be an enormously thick wedge: so thick that it threatens to split wide open the fundamental principles upon which our whole penal system is based—undermining the simple propositions . . . as to the responsibility of every sane adult for his own actions, as to his freedom to choose between good and evil and as to his liability to be punished should he prefer evil.

She questions very seriously whether the criminal law, as we know it, can survive the onslaught of new information from psychiatry. My distinguished friend Chief Justice Weintraub of the New Jersey Supreme Court foresees the same problem. He argues that if we allow the psychiatrist to define mental illness for us—and not restrict its legal meaning to knowledge of right and wrong—then he will soon tell us about the factors which affect human behavior. Soon expert witnesses would be testifying about psychological, economic, social, and other matters which cause or contribute to anti-social behavior.

Information about a defendant's mental disorder may then prove most troubling to the court in seeking a "just" disposition of his case—and may trouble society, too, by revealing that societal disorders contributed to individual disorder. Scientists now generally agree that human behavior is caused rather than willed, that man is most vulnerable in early life, that compared with other species he is capable of learning for an inordinately long period of his life, that he usually responds more readily to reward than to punishment, and that he learns more readily from his peers than from his masters.

What implications does this information have for our notions of individual responsibility and for our correctional systems? If the information science can give is deeply troubling to our methods of coping with offenders, does this justify us in ignoring it?

Here is a concrete example of the kind of dilemma we face. A few years ago, I served on President Kennedy's Panel on Mental Retardation. I received quite an education since I was the only lawyer in a group that included biologists, geneticists, educators, and psychiatrists. I learned from them for the first time that a disability—retardation, for instance—may arise from wholly unrelated causes, yet produce the same effects. Specifically, my panel colleagues told me, a man may act one way because he has a brain lesion—and we could all understand and forgive the act. But given the same external circumstances, another man may act the same way because of a failure of learning. One who is without identifiable brain damage may become functionally retarded if as an infant or young child he was deprived of a certain minimum of attention, social education, and intellectual stimulation. He will act the same way as the man with the brain lesion.

If this new information is valid, what happens to our notions of morality? Can we call one man responsible because he is "just plain dumb" and the other man not responsible because of brain damage? Can we continue to condemn people for ignorance? And if not, where does this leave the criminal law?

There is a related and somewhat less philosophical cause for resistance to new knowledge. Each lawyer, judge, and juror conceives his goal to be a decision. All he needs for this is the evidence. The clearer the evidence, the easier the decision. But psychiatry has not yet advanced (perhaps it never will) to the point where it can unequivocally specify what responsibility means. Opinion evidence—especially the opinions of behavioral scientists—is rarely given in black and white. Opinion is, after all, a balance of probabilities. But the psychiatrist sometimes finds this difficult to explain in court. Excerpts from a case transcript will show how a psychiatrist may be berated for inability to give a categorical answer to the prosecutor's questions:

> *Defense counsel on direct examination:* Would you state in your opinion whether there was a causal connection between the mental illness and the crime?
>
> *Doctor:* In my opinion, there probably was.
>
> *Court:* No, not probably. I want your expert opinion, not probability. Either you have an expert opinion or you do not.
>
> *Doctor:* Well, my expert opinion is I do not know for sure.
>
> *Court:* No, no. That doesn't answer the question.
>
> *Counsel:* Just give us your opinion—was there a causal connection between the crime and the mental disease?
>
> *Doctor:* I believe there was.
>
> *Court:* No. Not what you believe. You must answer the question, Doctor. He is asking for your expert opinion.
>
> *Counsel:* He said, "I believe there was." I think that is an honest answer.
>
> *Court:* That is begging the question. I want a direct answer.
>
> *Doctor:* Does your Honor mean Yes or No?
>
> *Court:* No, I mean that you must state your opinion. . . . State your expert opinion, not "I believe," or "I guess."
> . . . Now, I don't want any guessing. If you have an expert opinion, I want it.
>
> *Doctor:* Yes, my opinion is that the crime is probably

the product of illness.

Court: Not probably.

Counsel: We are not concerned with the word "probably." Can you give us your opinion?

Doctor: That is my opinion.

Court: That is not an opinion.

Doctor: I cannot answer Yes or No. I cannot answer it in terms of black and white.

Often the best kind of psychiatric evidence is "merely" opinion. It is an educated, knowledgeable, and often a logical and analytical judgment.

The decision-maker, whether judge or jury, is still left with the ancient and often agonizing tasks of evaluation, interpretation, and decision. In too many cases, the task of evaluation and interpretation are quickly abandoned, and the decision is reached by a much shorter route.

A short route to decision is to accept whichever expert gives the most clean-cut answers. It is the heart of my thesis that the M'Naghten rule encourages this spurious simplicity, while the facts of the sciences of behavior—at present— often lead toward uncertainty.

But if the law has not gone half-way to welcome behavioral science into the courtroom, neither have the psychiatrists faced up to their challenge.

What is usually required of the expert is a statement in simple terms of why the accused acted as he did—the psychodynamics of his behavior. In rare instances this is achieved. It occurs most often when the accused or his family has the money to employ a private expert to undertake the comprehensive study required. Then the psychiatrist will learn not only the factors that precipitated the behavior but how the accused became the sort of person he is, and how he must act. This, I repeat, is the exception. Where it occurs under the Durham rule, the accused may be seen as a sick person and confined to a hospital for treatment, not to a prison for punishment.

Of course it may not be possible for the psychiatrist—or any collection of witnesses—fully to explain *why* the accused acted as he did. The purpose of the Durham rule was to admit a wide range of complexity. But any point in that range, or any uncertainty, may be expressed with clarity.

The task of the expert witness is difficult. He must delve deep into the background of the accused. He must study, analyze, and co-ordinate physical, neurological, and psychological examinations. He must attempt to explain the whole man. He must provide the best explanation of the behavior. He cannot merely attach—or refuse to attach—a few labels or an IQ score. As our court emphasized in 1957:

> Unexplained medical labels—schizophrenia, paranoia, psychosis, neurosis, psychopathy—are not enough. . . . The chief value of an expert's testimony in this field, as in all other fields, rests upon the material from which his opinion is fashioned and the reasoning by which he progresses from his material to his conclusion . . . ; it does not lie in his mere expression of conclusion.

In a more recent case, I had occasion to make the harsh comment that:

> As far as the psychiatric testimony was concerned, [the defendants] might as well have been tried *in absentia*. They were not present in the conclusionary labels of the psychiatrists or in the perfunctory leading questions of counsel.

Why is the psychiatrist prone to give the court his diagnostic conclusion and little more? Basically, I often suspect, because he has little more to give. Our society will not divert enough of its resources to study those charged with crime. This goes to the root of our social system. Our psychiatrists may not be devoted entirely to the rich, but they certainly are seldom familiar with the poor. Most defendants charged with crimes of violence are poor, uneducated, deprived, and segregated. Socially and professionally, most psychiatrists are in the middle class. Psychotherapy has been called the therapy of communication. But many psychiatrists cannot communicate with those accused of crime—and too often they don't try.

Ignorance is compounded by the refusal to admit it. Doctors at one of our federal mental hospitals have often told me in private conversation that they do not have adequate staff and time to make thorough studies of the accused. But once in the courtroom they nevertheless try to live up to our expectations—they will not admit that they do not have all the answers. I sometimes feel that my psychiatrist friends who embrace Durham and then testify beyond their knowledge have done more to warp the Durham concept than the conservative lawyers who oppose it.

Enthusiastic psychiatrists often assume that *they* are being asked to make the moral and legal decision on guilt. They try to become lawyer, judge, jury, and society all rolled into one. They assume they "know" the law and what is good for society and for the accused. They give what we have begun to term "dispositional diagnoses."

Here is an example from a case which came before our court a few years ago. A man was indicted for arson. He gave such a complete written confession that even the police suggested he "was sick and needed psychiatric treatment." The confession revealed the classic symptoms of the sexual pyromaniac. He had been starting fires since he was 12 years old; he had set about 100 of them; the fire at which he had been apprehended was the second he had lit in that house that night.

A psychiatrist submitted the following written report—this and nothing more:

As a result of this examination and a previous examination . . . it is my opinion that the [accused] is of sound mind. Nothing is elicited which would lead me to the opinion that the act . . . was committed as a result of an irresistible impulse or otherwise as a result of mental illness.

The trial court accepted this report as submitted.

Some time after the appeal to our court was concluded, I met the psychiatrist—whom I knew quite well. I said to him, "John, you examined the pyromaniac—didn't you think he was sick?"

"Sure," he answered, "he was sick as hell."

"And dangerous," I pursued.

"Why, of course."

"Well, why did you tell the court he was of sound mind?"

"Because he was—well, he was not psychotic—he had no delusions or hallucinations—none of the symptomatology of psychosis."

Plainly, this psychiatrist believed that by some absolute legal fiat insanity means psychosis and nothing else. And even after I told him that such was not the law and that his report was therefore terribly misleading, he came forth with this clincher:

I think I would still limit my report to whether or not psychosis was present because it would be too difficult and uncertain to draw the line anywhere else.

Wittingly or not, he was writing the law.

I have been concerned principally with the behavioral scientists, the psychiatrists, and the psychologists who are now generally accepted as expert witnesses. But other fields are also contributing new knowledge about human behavior. The biologist, the geneticist, and the biochemist are making fantastic strides in developing information about human personality and the brain.

For a lawyer and a judge, I have had a unique opportunity to observe and participate in the discussions of some of these scientists. The initial (albeit perhaps misguided) enthusiasm for Durham either pulled or propelled me into their midst. I have not yet extricated myself. So I sit by and hear scientists explain the discovery of the genetic code. I hear them expound on the factors that affect how a human being will develop even before he is born. At the same time I learn that identical cells will act differently depending on the environment in which they are placed. These sciences are now bringing in clues to even more revolutionary findings, as far as ethics and law are concerned. The use of drugs to tranquilize or otherwise influence the mind will have far-reaching implications for our concepts of responsibility and justice.

Full of such facts and speculation, I come back from meetings with scientific groups at the Salk Institute for Biological Studies and various other institutions, and I try to concentrate on the cases which come before me for decision. But I must forget most of what I learned from the sciences of behavior when I judge the behavior of the real human beings who come before our courts.

It seems to me that the criminal law will find it harder and harder not to think about the science explosion. I sometimes wonder how long it will be before our orderly legal processes are shaken by our expanding knowledge of the human being and his behavior. And I wonder whether the biochemist will fare any better in the courtroom than his co-worker, the psychiatrist.

The relations between the individual and society cannot

be left to the scientists alone. The criminal law has a role to play. It enforces society's expectations. One might even say that the purpose of the criminal law has been to administer the effects of our disappointed expections. The law has traditionally sought to reduce the gap between society's expectations and the incapacity of some to fulfill them by minimizing recognition of that incapacity. M'Naghten seems designed to do precisely this. We put our expectations in one compartment and our learned sense of reality in another. There is little communication between the two. We are fearful that explanation may be taken as tolerance or absolution.

Yet my contention is the opposite. I contend that personal responsibility is linked—indeed locked—to understanding; and that as expectations are altered by growing knowledge, so a utilitarian morality will give way to a humane yet practical morality. A serious inquiry into the defendant's criminal responsibility can provide the catalyst for change.

That inquiry can be compared to a post mortem. The post mortem will not return the dead to life; the trial will not undo a heinous act. But in each case we can learn the causes of failure. And in the trial the entire community can learn—and thereby more clearly understand its responsibility for the act and for the redemption of the actor.

Admittedly the courtroom is not a scientific instrument. But our law libraries are actually man's greatest psychological archive of the natural history of human behavior. Psychological knowledge may reach mankind in many ways. To my mind, the courtroom can become one of the most incisive ways of explaining man and his failings to his fellow men. It can teach us yet again that "no man is an island"; that "though we are not all guilty, we are all responsible."

July/August 1967

FURTHER READING SUGGESTED BY THE AUTHOR:

Crime and the Criminal Law by Barbara Wootton (London: Stevens & Sons, 1963).

Psychoanalysis, Psychiatry and Law by Katz, Goldstein, Dershowitz (New York: The Free Press, 1967).

The Family and the Law by Goldstein and Katz (New York: The Free Press, 1965).

Insanity and the Criminal Law: From McNaghten to Durham, and Beyond by Simon E. Sobeloff (American Bar Association Journal—Vol. 41, September 1955).

President's Panel on Mental Retardation—Report of the Task Force on Law, January 1963, Library of Congress Catalogue Card No. 63-60030.

Juvenile Justice...
Quest and Realities

EDWIN M. LEMERT

The juvenile court is intended to succeed where parents have failed. But the family—even though disturbed by conflict, morally questionable, or broken by divorce or death—is the institution best suited for nurturing children into stable adults. Neither the Spartan *gymnasium,* nor the Russian *crèche,* nor the kibbutz nurseries, nor American orphanages, "homes," and reformatories can successfully duplicate the complex social and psychological construction of the family. Explicit recognition of this might well replace the pious injunction now in many laws that "care, custody, and discipline of children under the control of the juvenile court shall approximate that which they would receive from their parents."

In the majority opinion this May in *Gault v. Arizona,* which provided for some of the rights of criminal justice to be introduced into juvenile courts, Justice Abe Fortas pointedly wrote of the kind of care an incarcerated delinquent can expect from the state:

Instead of mother and father and sisters and brothers and friends and classmates, his world is peopled by guards, custodians, state employes, and "delinquents" confined with him for anything from waywardness to rape and homicide.

The harrassed juvenile court judge is not a father; a halfway house is not a home; a reformatory cell is not a teenager's bedroom; a hall counselor is not an uncle; and a cottage matron is not a mother. This does not mean that the system of children's justice should not seek kindly and dedicated people, but that it is a system with its own requirements. The judges, counselors, and matrons are permanent parts of the system; but their interests cannot be guaranteed to be the same as those of the children who are just passing through.

They do not pass through unmarked, however. An unwanted but unavoidable consequence to any child subjected to the system—including dependent and neglected children as well as delinquents—is the imposition of stigma. ("Dependent" refers to a residual category of nondelinquent children, such as orphans, for whom the state must take responsibility.) The necessary insight and social stamina to manage such stigma are not given to many people—least of all to the kind of children most likely to come into the juvenile court. Social rejections provoked by the stigma of wardship may convince the individual that he is "no good" or "can't make it on the outside." These beliefs may feed a brooding sense of injustice which leads to further delinquency.

An important rationale of state intervention is the faith that delinquency can be prevented and that the court can prevent it. The viability of this idea can be traced to a repressive Puritan psychology reinforced by the propaganda of the mental hygiene movement of the early twentieth century, which helped produce child guidance clinics, school social work, and juvenile courts. The metaphor is from medicine: High blood sugar warns of diabetes and a high cholesterol count is a warning of arteriosclerosis. In the early days of children's courts the comparable signs of juvenile delinquency were thought to be smoking and drinking, shining shoes, selling newspapers, or playing pool. The modern version is found in such ideas as pre-delinquent personality or delinquency proneness and in state laws which make truancy, running away from home, or incorrigibility bases for juvenile court control.

As yet, nothing has been isolated and shown to be a sure indicator of delinquency, nor is it likely that anything will be. Furthermore, things called "delinquent tendencies" often are found on close inspection to correspond not to any particular behavior, but rather to arbitrary definitions by school authorities, parents, and police. One investigation in New York found that, to a degree, truancy was simply a measure of the willingness or availability of parents to write excuses. Incorrigibility as found in juvenile court cases may mean anything from ignoring a mother's order not to see a boyfriend to assault with a deadly weapon—and often turns out to be parental neglect or unfitness.

The brave idea that the juvenile court can prevent delinquency is deflated or even reduced to absurdity by sociological studies of hidden delinquency which show that the majority of high school and college students at some time or another engage in delinquencies, not excluding serious law violations. The main difference between college students and youths who are made wards of juvenile courts is that the latter group contains more repeaters. While several interpretations are possible, these findings demand explanation. Why do youths who are made court wards commit more rather than fewer delinquencies? The conclusion that the court processing in some way helps to fix and perpetuate delinquency is hard to escape.

It must also be remembered that most youths pass through a time when they engage in delinquency. Children normally play hookey, help themselves to lumber from houses under construction, and snitch candy from dime stores; adolescent boys frequently swipe beer, get drunk, "borrow" cars, hell around, learn about sex from available females or prostitutes, or give the old man a taste of his own medicine. Transitional deviance not only is ubiquitous in our society but universal to all societies, especially among boys turning into men—Margaret Meade's droll observations on adolescence in the South Seas to the contrary notwithstanding.

Most youths outgrow their socalled predelinquency and their law flouting; they put away childish things as they become established in society by a job, marriage, further education, or by the slow growth of wisdom. Maturation out of the deviance of adolescence is facilitated when troublesome behavior, even petty crime, is dealt with by parents, neighbors, and policemen, and treated as a manifestation of the inevitable diversity, perversity, and shortcomings of human beings—in other words, as a problem of everyday living calling for tolerable solutions, not perfection. This means the avoidance whenever possible of specialized or categorical definitions which invidiously differentiate, degrade, or stigmatize persons involved in the problems. The cost of muddling through with children who become problems have multiplied with the rising plateau of mass conformities needed for a high-energy society, but they must be absorbed in large part where the alternatives are even more costly.

The ideology of delinquency prevention is much more urban than rural. Handling problems of youthful disorders and petty crime in rural areas and small towns—characteristically by sheriff's deputies, town police, the district attorney, and the probation officer—has been largely informal. Sharp distinctions are drawn between less consequential moral and legal infractions—"Mickey Mouse stuff"—and serious delinquencies, with no implication that one leads to the other. This is reflected in the reluctance of elective officials and those beholden to them to make records of their actions, but at the same time they want action in serious misdemeanors and felonies by youth to be swift and punitive. The juvenile court usually reserves formal action for "real problems" of families and the community; the functional context of youthful misconduct ordinarily can be realistically gauged and its consequences dealt with in a number of different situations.

A major difficulty in the bureaucratic urban juvenile court is that the functional context of child problems directed to it easily gets lost; it has to be reconstructed by bits and pieces of information obtained through investigations and inquiries conducted under highly artificial circumstances and communicated in series of stereotyped written reports. There is little or no direct community criticism or reaction that might put individual cases into a common-sense context. This plus the rapidity with which cases are heard in large courts (three minutes per case in Los Angeles in 1959) explains why the distinction between trivia and serious child problems breaks down. A notorious illustration came to light in Orange County, California, in 1957 when a private attorney put his own investigator to work on a case of an eight-year-old boy and a nine-year-old girl accused of a "sex crime" against a seven-year-old girl. He found that the case had been presented in court by a probation officer who was only repeating without investigation what he had been told. This private inquiry pared the charge down to an imputed incident witnessed by no one and reported two days after it supposedly occurred.

It would push facts too far to insist that the ideology of preventing delinquency is used by juvenile court workers and judges to justify slipshod operations. Nevertheless, it has allowed them to change the basis of jurisdiction from one "problem" to another. The practice is baldly indicated in the statement of a California judge arguing for retention under juvenile court jurisdiction of simple traffic violations by juveniles:

> Moreover it seems to have been demonstrated that the broad powers of the juvenile court can be helpfully invoked on behalf of children whose maladjustment has been brought to light through juvenile traffic violations. A girl companion of a youthful speeder may be protected from further sexual [sic] experimentation. Boys whose only amusement seems to be joyriding in family cars can be directed to other more suitable forms of entertainment before they reach the stage of "borrowing" cars when the family car is unavailable.

The police generally are less concerned with the prevention of delinquency in individual cases than with prevention and control in the community as manifested in gang violence, disturbances of public order, a rise in crime rates, or mounting property losses. The utility of specious legal categories describing delinquent tendencies is most obvious when the police seek to break up youthful gang activity, quell public disturbances such as occur at drive-ins or public parks, or seek access to witnesses or informants to solve a crime or to recover stolen property. While the arrest and detention of youth to "clear up other crimes" may be efficient police tactics, abuses may arise at the expense of individual youths if such methods can be pursued under diffuse charges. Unfortunately there have been and are judges willing to allow juvenile detention to be used for these purposes. It was for these reasons that the Juvenile Justice Commission of California, following a statewide survey, recommended in 1960 the use of citations for minor offenses by juveniles, and the requirement that detention hearings be held within specified time limits to act as a check on overzealous police action.

It is true that, in a number of areas, the police have sought to aid juveniles to avoid clashes with the law through setting up recreation programs, "big brother" assignments, systems of referral to welfare agencies, informal probation, and even police social work. But such undertakings have declined in recent years and tend to be looked upon as divergent from essential police functions such as apprehension of criminals, recovery of property, and maintenance of public order. This may also point to growing police disillusionment with more generalized or community delinquency prevention programs. Police in some cities sharply disagree with community organizers of such projects over the issue of maintaining the autonomy of neighborhood gangs. They take a jaundiced view of attempts to divert such groups into more compliant pursuits, preferring rather to break them up.

Research assessments of community programs to prevent delinquency—such as the Chicago Area Project, the Harlem Project, and the Cambridge-Somerville Youth Study—have been disappointing; results either have been negative or inconclusive. Possible exceptions are community coordinating councils, especially in the Western United States where they originated. These councils bring police, probation officers, judges, and social workers together in face-to-face discussions of local youth problems. However, they seem to work best in towns between 2,000 and 15,000 population; it remains unclear whether they can be adapted successfully to large urban areas. Significantly, they work chiefly by exchanging agency information and referrals of cases to community agencies, with full support and cooperation of the police. In effect they represent concerted action to bypass the juvenile court, and it might be said that their purpose, if not function, is prevention of delinquency by preventing, wherever possible, the adjudication of cases in the court.

Much of what has already been said about preventing delinquency through the juvenile court is equally applicable to therapeutic treatment through the court. The ideal of treatment found its way into juvenile court philosophy from social work and psychiatry. Its pervasiveness is measurable by the extent to which persons educated and trained in social work have indirectly influenced the juvenile court or moved into probation and correction. A premise of therapeutic treatment of children is that scientific knowledge and techniques make possible specific solutions to problems.

Scientific social work has come to lean heavily on Freudian theories. Updated versions of socially applied psychoanalysis conceive of delinquency as an acting out of repressed conflicts in irrational, disguised forms. The accent is on internal emotional life rather than upon external acts: The social worker or the psychiatrist is a specialist who understands the problems while the client does not; the specialist "knows best," studies, analyzes, and treats— much in the manner of the authoritative medical practitioner.

A divergent, competing line of thought in social work repudiates scientific treatment in favor of a simpler task of helping, in which problems are confronted in whatever terms the child or youth presents them; responsible involvement of the client is a sine qua non of success in this process.

Generally speaking, social workers advocate assigning to other agencies many of the tasks the court has assumed. Some social workers seriously doubt whether the helping process can be carried on in an authoritarian setting, and to emphasize their stand refuse as clients children who have been wards of the court. Other social workers believe that judges should not go beyond their competence, but should use their power solely for adjudication, with determination of treatment left to social work agencies. A smaller number of social workers hold to a more sanguine view of reconciling personal help and authority within the role of the probation officer. Finally, there are some social workers who are not above using juvenile court power as a tool for getting access to clients or prolonging their contacts with them because they will "benefit from treatment." This pattern became aggravated in Utah when juvenile courts were under the administrative control of the state department of welfare.

Actually, comparatively few juvenile court cases are referred to social workers for treatment, and many juvenile court judges and probation officers are hostile to social workers. According to a U.S. Children's Bureau study, the most frequent disposition of juvenile court cases was dismissal; next was informal or formal supervision by a probation officer. Dismissals can scarcely be called treatment, even though the associated court appearance before an admonitory judge may have a chastening effect upon some youths. At most, such cases feature a brief exchange with an investigating officer who asks some questions, issues a stern warning, and says he hopes he will not see the boy again.

The consequences of supervision of delinquents by probation officers have been little studied and the outcome, even when successful, little understood. Probation practices with juveniles have little in common across the nation, and often they consist of a meager combination of office interviews and phone or mail reports. Probation officers frequently claim that they could give more help to their charges if they had more time, but this must be regarded as an occupational complaint rather than an accurate prediction. What little experimental research there is on the subject shows that mere reduction of the size of caseloads of probation and parole officers does not in itself lower rates of recidivism. More time to deal with their client's problems is a necessary, but not a sufficient, condition of success by court workers.

If the results of probation supervision of delinquents on the whole are disappointing or inconclusive, even less can be said in behalf of the treatment of juvenile offenders in institutions. Sociological analysis and evaluations of such correctional programs tend to be negative. Some writers even say that the goals of correctional programs in prisons and reformatories are inherently self-defeating. This follows from the very fact of incarceration, which by imposing personal deprivation on inmates generates hostility to formal programs of rehabilitation. Furthermore, the population of repeaters shapes inmate socialization.

The problems of juvenile correction and rehabilitation have been highlighted in the popular press and literature as poor physical plants, meager appropriations, and underpaid, undereducated personnel, but they lie far deeper. It remains doubtful whether even the generously funded and well-staffed California Youth Authority has neared its original purpose of providing individualized treatment for youthful offenders. This cannot be traced to lack of dedication in the leadership, but to the task of administering the institutions, where bureaucratic values and organizational inertia conspire daily to defeat the purpose of treatment. These dilemmas have led the CYA to begin establishing community treatment projects on a large scale and subsidizing probation programs with the hope of stimulating local innovation of alternatives to incarceration.

I do not mean to exclude the possibility that clinically trained and humanly wise people can help youth solve problems which have brought them athwart the law. Rather the intent is to leaven professional pretense with humility, to place the notion of treatment in a more realistic perspective, and to point out the differences between dealing with problems of human relationships and treatment as it has evolved in the practice of medicine. The treatment of delinquency is best regarded as a kind of guidance, special education, and training—much more akin to midwifery than medicine—in which hopeful intervention into an ongoing process of maturation is undertaken. The judge, probation officer, correctional counselor, or institutional psychiatrist can be at most a small influence among the many affecting development and emergence into adulthood. Although the juvenile court can determine that certain influences will take place in a prescribed order in the process of socialization, it cannot control the meanings and values assigned to such occurrences.

If there is a defensible philosophy for the juvenile court, it is one of judicious nonintervention. It is properly an agency of last resort for children, holding to the analogy of appeal courts, where all other remedies must be exhausted before a case will be considered. This means that problems accepted for action by the juvenile court will be demonstrably serious by testable evidence ordinarily distinguished by a history of repeated failures at solutions by parents, relatives, schools, and community agencies. The model should be the English and Canadian juvenile courts, which receive very few cases by American standards.

This statement of juvenile court philosophy rests upon the following propositions:

■ Since the powers of the juvenile court are extraordinary, properly it should deal with extraordinary cases.

■ Large numbers of cases defeat the purposes of the juvenile court by leading to bureaucratic procedures inimical to individual treatment.

■ The juvenile court is primarily a court of law and must accept limitations imposed by the inapplicability of rule and remedy to many important phases of human conduct and to some serious wrongs. Law operates by punishment, injunction against specific acts, specific redress, and substitutional redress. It cannot by such means make a father good, a mother moral, a child obedient, or a youth respectful of authority.

■ When the juvenile court goes beyond legal remedies, it must resort to administrative agents, or itself become such an agency. This produces conflicts and confusion of values and objectives. Furthermore, it remains problematic whether child and parental problems can be solved by administrative means.

It may be protested that here I am narrowing the conception of the juvenile court severely and that my model can hardly be recognized as a juvenile court at all by present standards.

However, organized nonintervention by the juvenile courts can become a definite protection for youth. Children need as much or more protection from the unanticipated consequences of organized movements, programs, and services in their behalf as they need from the formless "evils" which gave birth to the juvenile court. America no longer has a significant number of Fagins, exploiters of child labor, sweatshops, open saloons, houses of prostitution, street trades, immoral servants, cruel immigrant fathers, traveling carnivals and circuses, unregulated race tracks, much open gambling, or professional crime of the old style. The battles for compulsory education have long since been won, and technological change has eliminated child labor—perhaps too well. The forms of delinquency have changed as the nature of society has changed; social and personal problems of youth reflect the growth of affluence in one area of society and the growth of hostility and aggression in a nonaffluent sector. Current sociological theories of delinquency, stress as "causes" drift and risk-taking, on the one hand, and dilapidated opportunity structures, on the other.

The basic life process today is one of adaptation to exigencies and pressures; individual morality has become functional rather than sacred or ethical in the older sense. To recognize this at the level of legislative and judicial policy is difficult because social action in America always has been heavily laden with moral purpose. However, if the juvenile court is to become effective, its function must be reduced to enforcement of the "ethical minimum" of youth conduct necessary to maintain social life in a high-energy, consuming, pluralistic society. It can then proceed to its secondary task of arranging the richest possible variety of assistance to those specially disadvantaged children and youth who come under its jurisdiction.

A philosophy of judicious nonintervention demands more than verbal or written exhortation for implementation. Action is needed to reshape the juvenile court. Ideally it will be so structured that it will have built-in controls, feedback mechanisms, and social scanning devices which make it self-regulating and adaptive. This by no means signifies that the juvenile court should or will become "inner directed"; if anything, contacts and interaction with the community and its agencies will have more importance, if for no other reason than to protect its stance of nonintervention.

Relationships between juvenile courts and policing agencies probably will become more critical with a shrinkage in juvenile court functions. However, it can be hoped that this will be an irritant leading more police departments to develop juvenile bureaus and to upgrade their competence for screening and adjusting cases within the department. Even now it is common practice for police departments to dismiss large numbers of juvenile arrests or "adjust" them within the department. More and better juvenile officers and rational procedures can greatly decrease referrals to juvenile courts. This does not mean that police will undertake probation or social work, but rather will parsimoniously work with relatives and community agencies, or at most will engage in brief, policemanlike counseling with youths whom they believe they can help.

Since the police will never entirely forsake their habit of using the juvenile court for their own special purpose of keeping law and order, the second line of defense for judicious nonintervention must be the intake workers of the court or probation department. Ideally, the most competent workers would be organized into a fairly autonomous division of intake, referral, and adjustment, which would be oriented toward community agencies and given the prerogative of denying petitions for court jurisdiction.

As has been noted, referral of cases from juvenile courts to social work agencies is complicated because the agencies do not want to work with hostile or uncooperative clients.

Juvenile courts trying to treat children with small difficulties—often indistinguishable from those being handled
in large numbers by welfare agencies—lose the chance to
refer them to the agencies later. For this reason, referrals
should be made immediately—no detention, no confrontation with child or parent, no detailed investigation. The
court intake procedure should not be turned into a fishing
expedition to uncover and record "problems" to justify
further court action.

In general, juvenile courts are granted control over dependent and neglected, as well as delinquent, children.
Despite the early aim of the juvenile court to take stigma
away from these statuses, the pall of moral questionability
settles over all court wards in spite of category.

It is virtually impossible to defend the court's jurisdiction
over dependent children on any grounds but convenience.
Just why, for example, a child whose mother has been
committed to a mental institution should be made the ward
of a latently criminal court is not readily explainable. The
same is true for children whose parents are troubled by
unemployment or illness, and likewise for orphaned or
illegitimate children. Granted that they need protection
with legal sanction, there is no proof that the civil courts
cannot entrust this job to the welfare agencies, assuming
full protection of the rights of parents and children. Some
probation officers find justification for juvenile court jurisdiction where some children in a family are delinquent and
others merely dependent. But there is as much justification
in such cases for allowing civil agencies jurisdiction over
all but the most seriously delinquent children.

The arguments for supervision of neglected children by
juvenile courts are only slightly more forceful. If the
child's problem is truly the fault of his parents, why should
the child be branded? The suspicion is strong that juvenile

courts are used to gain control over children where the proof of parental neglect is too flimsy to stand scrutiny in an adult criminal court. It is a knotty problem, admittedly, but children should not be paying the costs of official indirection. If the parents can be shown in a general court to be at fault, let the custody of the children go to a welfare agency if necessary. If the parents cannot be shown to be at fault, let the matter end.

At the root of this desire to keep dependent and neglected children under the eye of the court is the persistent belief that crime and delinquency are caused by dependency and neglect. This idea, descended from hoary biblical notions and Victorian moralism, still turns up, as in the description of the dependency and neglect unit in the recent annual report of an urban probation department:

> Implicit in the function of this unit is the concept that it is very probable that the basis for delinquent acting has been laid in the children and that delinquency prevention is, therefore, a primary concern.

Little durable evidence has been discovered to support the contention that poverty, broken homes, or parental failures—alcoholism, sexual immorality, or cruelty—are in themselves causes of delinquency. Most delinquents come from intact homes, and there is little unanimity on whether broken homes produce more than their proportional share of delinquents. Furthermore, every delinquent from a broken home averages two or more brothers and sisters who are not delinquent.

If we are to have judicious nonintervention, then we cannot continue to have statutory jurisdiction defined in such subjective fashion. Given the untoward consequences of labeling, we cannot continue to work under diffuse definitions which allow almost any child, given compromising circumstances, to be caught up in the net of the court.

When such specious legal grounds as incorrigibility, truancy, and running away from home are warrants for juvenile court action, they allow parents, neighbors, school officials, and police—even the youths themselves—to solve their problems by passing them on to the court. Note, for instance, the lengthy conflict between juvenile court workers and school officials, in which the school people are accused of foisting off their own failures on the court. The educators reply heatedly that the court is unreceptive or does nothing about "really mean kids." Probation officers ruefully discover in some counties that sheriff's deputies expect them to settle all neighborhood quarrels in which juveniles are involved. Parents or relatives many times make it clear in court that they desire their child to be punished for highly personal reasons. A depressing sidelight is that the court itself can be a cause for incorrigibility. Failure to obey an order of the court can be an official reason for severe punishment, even though the original excuse for taking jurisdiction may have been minor.

Runaways must be understood in the same context as incorrigibles, with the added difference that they are more frequently girls. Often running away is a dramatic demonstration—a little like suicide attempts by adult women. California girls sometimes demand to be placed in detention in order to expose the "hatefulness" of their homes or to embarrass their parents. While police action often is clearly indicated for runaways, action by the court is decidedly not. If drama is needed, it should be staged under some other auspices.

Incorrigibility, truancy, and running away should not be in themselves causes for court jurisdiction. The social agencies are well equipped to handle such problems. In fact, an inquiry in the District of Columbia showed that agencies were handling 98 percent of the runaways, 95 percent of the truants, 76 percent of the juvenile sex offenses, and 46 percent of the incorrigibles.

Much has been said of the "philosophy" of the juvenile court and little can be added, other than to note that this very preoccupation with philosophy sets it apart from other courts. In general, American courts for children have been given broad legislative grants to help and protect children, to depart from strict rules of legal procedure, and to utilize what in other courts is excluded evidence. One result has been that, under the noble guise of humanitarian concern and scientific treatment, the courts have often simply deprived the children of justice and fair play. The juvenile court originated in humanitarian concern rather than the police powers of the state, and legislators are disposed to treat it as a child welfare agency. Thus, few procedures were specified in early statutes. Later accretions in statutes and common law have proved to be extremely divergent, and little in the way of case law developed, particularly since it took until the 1960's for the first juvenile court appeal to reach the Supreme Court of the United States.

Inattention to procedure has led to the absence of hard rules on hearings, with the result that in many courts hearings are attenuated, ambiguously accusatory, or even nonexistent. Thus, the least we can ask of judicious nonintervention is that a hearing be given any child whose freedom is likely to be abridged by the court. A further desirable change would be the introduction of split hearings: one devoted to factual findings rich enough to justify taking jurisdiction, and one to ascertain what should be done with the child. Both hearings should be rigorous, but the second should admit social data which might make clear the reasons for the delinquent act. This procedure will prevent the

court from taking jurisdiction on the basis of impression-
istic hearsay evidence, but will also allow such evidence to
help the judge make the punishment fit not the crime, but
the criminal. This division should be made most clear, for
studies of split hearings in New York and California have
showed that about two-thirds of the judges continued to
read social reports before asserting jurisdiction, thus de-
feating the purpose of the split hearings. Appellate courts
in California feel the social report is germane to adjudication; those in New York do not. Instead of more opinions,
we should set about finding out whether the minority judges
in these two states, as well as all English juvenile court
judges, are hampered by the absence of this information in
asserting jurisdiction.

Wherever the social report is admitted in the process, it
should be subject to scrutiny. This implies the presence of
lawyers for the prosecution and defense. In its decision in
the Gault case this May, the Supreme Court assured the
presence of defense lawyers, a practice which has been
followed for several years in California, New York, Minnesota, and the District of Columbia. The traditional argument against this practice, which was used by Justice
Potter Stewart in his dissent in Gault, is that the introduction of counsel may rob the juvenile court of its informal
ad hoc quality and turn it into little more than a miniature
criminal court. My own California studies indicate that
advising parents and children of the right to counsel, as
ordered by the legislature in 1961, has increased the statewide use of counsel from 3 percent of the cases to 15 percent. In some counties, the rise was from 0 to 1 or 2 percent; in others it was from 15 percent to 70 or even 90
percent. In assigning counsel, the courts have favored dependent or neglected children and those charged with
serious offenses. I have found no indication of racial or

social discrimination in assignments.

One problem that has emerged is that private attorneys tend to lack knowledge of the system and regularly assigned public defenders tend to get wired into it. In both instances, the client may be hurt. Mere introduction of counsel seems insufficient to guarantee judicious nonintervention if the intake of cases is not reduced.

Introduction of defense counsel has not automatically meant introduction of prosecutors. The presentation of the state's case has fallen in many instances to the probation officer, who lacks both the training and the temperament to prosecute. He knows that active prosecution will later make it difficult or impossible to help the child. Where a judge takes over the interrogation, defense attorneys may be left in the untenable position of objecting to his questions and then hearing him rule on the objections. The police are more enthusiastic about placing prosecutors in the courts than the prosecutors are, and judges are not yet disposed to permit hearings to become all-out adversary struggles. Their attitude is not ill considered. I have seen an attorney in such a situation attempt to attack the credibility of a witness—a 15-year-old girl—by bringing her juvenile record into court and referring to sexual experiences for which she received money.

My research has shown that cases with attorneys are more likely to be dismissed, less likely to result in wardship, and more likely to end in a suspended sentence than cases without an attorney. The dismissals were not evenly distributed among the delinquent, the dependent, and the neglected children, however; the cases of neglected children—that is, those actions alleging unfit homes—were the ones most frequently dismissed. Attorneys were often successful in attacking imprecise charges and having them reduced. Attorneys were also able to negotiate alternative dispositions of cases, such as finding relatives to take a child rather than sending him to a foster home, proposing psychiatric help rather than commitment to a ranch school, or sometimes convincing the client that cooperation with the probation officer is preferable to resistance and ending with loss of parental control. If these findings are indicative, the adversary function is likely to be marginal in relation to the attorney's function as a negotiator and interpreter between the judge and family. Of course, the very likelihood of an attorney entering cases has a monitory value in reinforcing the new consciousness of court workers regarding the rights of juveniles. The New York concept of the attorney as a law guardian seems most fitting.

The interest in the role of attorneys in the juvenile court has brought about a concern with the sort of evidence to be accepted and the levels of proof required. The judges I have studied in California deal with the problem of hearsay evidence by admitting everything, on the assumption that they can consider only the competent evidence. This view has some support in legal opinion, where it is argued that the hearsay rule was aimed at controlling gullible juries rather than judges. But in the juvenile court much evidence is in the form of reports which are little more than compilations of professional hearsay; whether the ordinary judge is always qualified to sift this sort of evidence is questionable. Many judges seem remarkably naive about evaluating psychiatric and social science reports.

In civil courts—where only property is at stake—a preponderance of evidence is sufficient to decide the case. Considering the nature of the evidence in juvenile court, however, this may be insufficient. I would suggest that clear and convincing proof, that which admits only one conclusion, be the standard for determining guilt. For the most grievous juvenile crimes, the standard of criminal proof, guilt beyond all reasonable doubt, should prevail, as it does, for example, in English juvenile courts.

Although the justices did not discuss standards of evidence and proof explicitly in the Gault case, they did apply standards of adult courts in the right to counsel, the protection against self-incrimination, the right of confrontation and cross-examination, and the right to timely and explicit notice of the charges. Altogether, this is a strong indication that the extensive use of hearsay will not be viewed lightly when and if the Supreme Court is called upon to rule on standards of evidence and proof.

The words of the court in *Kent v. United States,* the first juvenile court case it ever heard, characterize the present state of affairs:

There is evidence, in fact, that there may be grounds for concern that the child receives the worst of both worlds; that he gets neither the protections accorded to adults nor the solicitous care and regenerative treatment postulated for children.

The doctrine of judicious nonintervention is nothing more than a plea that the child in court be granted the best of both worlds. Welcome as the Gault decision is in granting some of the protections accorded to adults, until some attempt is made to stem the flow of cases into the juvenile courts, solicitous care and regenerative treatment may be impossible.

July/August 1967

FURTHER READING SUGGESTED BY THE AUTHOR:

Justice for the Child edited by Margaret K. Rosenheim (Glencoe, Illinois: Free Press, 1962) A collection of critical essays raising questions of the quality of justice in juvenile courts.

The Juvenile Courts by F. T. Gile (London: George Allen and Unwin Ltd., 1946). A highly readable discussion of the work and problems of English juvenile courts, with some tart things to say about their American counterparts.

Pornography-
Raging Menace or Paper Tiger?

WILLIAM SIMON/JOHN H. GAGNON

Since the task of defining pornography has fallen more and more on the Supreme Court—and since not much research exists on what effect pornography has on the social actions of individuals—what standard is the court using?

The Supreme Court seems to be erecting a more complex standard for judging pornography to replace the old concern with individual morality. Some interesting insights into the confusion surrounding the topic can be drawn from three court decisions of March 21, 1966: *Ginzburg* v. *United States, Mishkin* v. *New York,* and *Memoirs of a Woman of Pleasure* v. *Massachusetts.* Although this set of decisions was almost immediately accorded distinction as a landmark by the public, the Nine Old Men themselves did not seem quite so sure of the meaning of the affair. The justices produced among them 14 separate opinions in the three cases. Only three judges were in the majority in

163

all cases. The decisions were divided, respectively, 5-4, 6-3, and 6-3.

Ginzburg is the key decision. The court reversed the suppression of *Memoirs,* better known as *Fanny Hill,* under the Roth test of 1957—that is, "whether to the average person, applying contemporary standards, the dominant theme of the material taken as a whole appeals to a prurient interest." The conviction of Edward Mishkin, owner of the Main Stem and Midget book stores in New York City, was upheld. In the words of the court, Mishkin "was not prosecuted for anything he said or believed, but for what he did." What he did was commission, publish, and sell such illustrated books as *Mistress of Leather, Cult of Spankers,* and *Fearful Ordeal in Restraintland* for an audience interested in sadomasochism, transvestitism, fetishism.

Ralph Ginzburg was being tried on postal charges of obscenity for three publications: *The Housewife's Handbook of Selective Promiscuity,* an issue of the biweekly newsletter *Liaison,* and a volume of the hardbound magazine *Eros.* In this case the court departed from earlier rulings by considering not the obscenity of the specific items, but rather the appeal to prurient interest made in the advertising campaigns. The court remarked, "Where the purveyor's sole emphasis is on the sexually provocative aspects of his publications, that fact may be decisive in the determination of 'obscenity.'"

To the court, one of the proofs of Ginzburg's motives was his request for second-class mailing privileges at Intercourse or Blue Ball, Pennsylvania, before obtaining them at Middlesex, New Jersey. One of the indicators of the social worth of *Fanny Hill,* conversely, was the translation of the book into braille by the Library of Congress.

Three of the justices voting for reversal filed written dissents in which they argued that the court was creating a new crime—that of pandering, exploitation, or titillation—which Ginzburg could not have known existed when he committed it. Furthermore, the dissenters said, if a statute creating such a crime had come before the court, it would be found unconstitutional.

It is the Ginzburg decision that gives us the primary thread to follow in seeking to understand "obscenity" as it is now seen by the Supreme Court and the sexual arousal caused by what is conventionally termed pornography. With this decision the court has moved—in a way that may be inimical to the conception of law as abstract principle—toward a more realistic determination of the factors relevant to triggering a sexual response. The court's sociological discovery—whether intentional or not—is that in sex the context of the representation is significant. That is, sex as a physical object or symbolic representation has no power outside a context in which the erotic elements are reinforced or made legitimate.

In doing this, the court did not change the rules under which any work will be considered outside its context. If a book is charged—as *Fanny Hill* was—with being obscene under the Roth decision, it will be treated in exactly the same way as it would have been in the past. When aspects of the context of advertising or sale—the acts of labeling—are included in the original charges, then the Ginzburg rules will be applied. This was demonstrated in the court's decision this May on a number of girlie magazines. Obscenity convictions against the magazines were overturned because, as the court stated, "In none was there evidence of the sort of pandering which the court found significant in *Ginzburg v. United States*."

Whether the majority of the court was aware of the significance of the change it made in the definition of obscenity is not clear. From the tone of the opinions, it is obvious the court felt it was dealing with a problem of nuisance behavior—not only to the public, but to the court itself—quite analogous to keeping a goat in a residential area, or urinating in public. By making the promotion of the work a factor in determining its obscenity, the court was reinforcing the right of the person to keep his mailbox clean and private, not to mention the likelihood that it was cutting down the amount of misleading advertising.

The court apparently considers pornography to have two major dimensions. The first can be defined as dealing with sexual representations that are offensive to public morality or taste, which concerned the court most importantly in the Ginzburg case. The second centers on the effect of pornography on specific individuals or classes, which is the focus of most public discussions and prior court decisions on pornography. This dimension was mentioned only twice in the array of decisions of 1966, but much of the confusion in discussions of pornography reflects a difficulty in distinguishing between these dimensions or a tendency to slip from one to the other without noting the change.

The first dimension—offenses to a public morality—not only appears more objective, but also has a cooler emotional tone. The problem becomes one of tolerating a public nuisance, or defining what constitutes a public nuisance. This issue becomes complex because the heterogeneity of an urban society makes it difficult to arrive at a consensus on what the limits of public morality might be. We might also add the complicating factor of our society's somewhat uneven libertarian tradition that affirms the theoretical existence of the right to subscribe to minority versions of morality. These obviously touch upon important issues of constitutional freedoms. As important as the implicit issues may be, however, the explicit issue is public nuisance, a misdemeanor, usually bringing only a fine or, at most, up to a year in the county jail. Talk of offense to public morality or public taste is relatively remote from the old fears of serious damage to the community or its members.

The second dimension—effects upon persons exposed to pornographic productions—generates more intense emotions. Claims are made that exposure to pornography results in infantile and regressive approaches to sexuality that can feed an individual's neuroses or, at the other extreme, that exposure tends to fundamentally and irreversibly corrupt and deprave. The latter argument asserts that exposure to pornography either awakens or creates sexual appetites that can only be satisfied through conduct that is dangerous to society. More simply stated: Pornography is a trigger mechanism that has a high probability of initiating dangerous, antisocial behavior. There also exists what can be called a major counterargument to these, but one that shares with them a belief in the effectiveness of pornography. This argument is that pornography serves as an alternative sexual outlet, one that releases sexual tensions that might otherwise find expression in dangerous, antisocial behavior. For the proponents of this view, pornography is seen as a safety valve or a psychological lightning rod.

The very act of labeling some item as pornographic or obscene creates a social response very close to that brought on by pornography itself. The act of labeling often generates sexual anticipation centered on fantasies about the business of pornography and the erotic character of those who produce it. How else could such benign and hardly erotic productions as family-planning pamphlets and pictures of human birth have come under the shadow of the pornography laws? As with other unconventional sexual expressions, in public consideration of pornography even the dreary details of production, distribution, and sale are matters for erotic speculation. This simplification—defining as totally sexual that which is only marginally connected with sexuality—is perhaps one of the major sources of the public concern over pornography.

Labeling can also be done by individuals, who can thus make pornographic the widest range of materials—*Studs Lonigan, Fanny Hill, Playboy,* the Sears Roebuck catalog. This ability leads to the assumption that sexual fantasy and its agent, pornography, have a magical capacity to commit men to overt sexual action. In this view the sexual impulse lies like the beast in every man, restrained only by the slight fetters of social repression. This assumption, founded on the Enlightenment's notion of a social contract, underpins most of our discussions of sex and its sideshow, pornography.

These serious views of pornography can lead directly to the formulation of an empirically testable question. Unfortunately, no one has provided an answer acceptable as the outcome of reliable and systematic research procedures.

Of the data that are available on the effects of pornography, the best remain those provided by the investigations of the Institute for Sex Research. Kinsey and his associates indicate that the majority of males in our society are exposed, at one time or another, to "portrayals of sexual action." So are a smaller proportion of females. Further, 77 percent of males who had exposure to "portrayals of sexual action" reported being erotically aroused, while only 32 percent of women reported feelings of arousal. What is significant is that, arousal notwithstanding, no dramatic changes of behavior appeared to follow for those reporting both exposure and arousal. Perhaps even more significant is the fact that Paul H. Gebhard and his colleagues in their book *Sex Offenders* report:

> It would appear that the possession of pornography does not differentiate sex offenders from nonsex offenders. Even the combination of ownership plus strong sexual

arousal from the material does not segregate the sex offender from other men of a comparable social level. Summing up their feeling that pornography is far from being a strong determinant of sexual behavior and that the use of pornography tends to be a derivative of already existing sexual commitments, the authors observe: "Men make the collections, collections do not make the men."

However, given the intensity and frequency with which the argument of pornography's corrupting powers is raised, one might wonder whether thinking about pornography has not itself given rise to sexual fantasies, developing an image of men and women as being more essentially sexual than they may in fact be.

The two major dimensions—public offense versus public corruption—result in two different images of the pornographer. Projected through the rhetoric of public corruption we see him as someone self-consciously evil, a representative of the antichrist, the Communist conspiracy, or at the very least, the Mafia. We also tend to see him in terms of the obscenity of ill-gotten wealth as he deals in commodities that are assumed to generate high prices.

Thought of as a public nuisance, he appears in somewhat more realistic hues. Here we find not a sinister villain but a grubby businessman producing a minor commodity for which there is a limited market and a marginal profit and which requires that he live in a marginal world. Here our collective displeasure may be derived from his association with a still greater obscenity—economic failure. However, whether the pornographer is Mephistopheles or a Willie Loman, he is one of the few in our society whose public role is overtly sexual, and that is perhaps reason enough to abandon any expectations of rationality in public discussions of the role.

We tend to ignore the social context within which pornography is used and from which a large part of its significance for the individual consumer derives. The stag film is an excellent case in point. Out of context it is rarely more than a simple catalogue of the limited sexual resources of the human body. Stag films are rarely seen by females and most commonly by two kinds of male groups: those living in group housing in colleges or universities and those belonging to upper-lower class and lower-middle class voluntary social groups. The stag film serves both similar and different functions for the two major categories of persons who see them.

For the college male they are a collective representation of mutual heterosexual concerns and—to a lesser degree—they instruct in sexual technique. For this group the exposure is either concurrent with, or prior to, extensive sociosexual experience. Exposure comes later in life for the second group: after marriage or, at the very least, after the development of sociosexual patterns. For this audience the group experience itself provides validation of sexual appetites in social milieus where other forms of validation, such as extramarital activity, are severely sanctioned. The films primarily reinforce masculinity and only indirectly reinforce heterosexuality. This reinforcement of heterosexuality is reflected in the way the films portray the obsessive myths of masculine sexual fantasy. They emphasize, for example, that sexual encounters can happen at any moment, to anyone, around almost any corner—a belief that is a close parallel to the romantic love fantasy so very characteristic of female arousal. In the case of the male, however, sex replaces love as the central element. These films also reaffirm the myth of a breed of women who are lusty and free in both surrender and enjoyment. Last, given the kind of social context within which the films are shown, there is little reason to assume that their sexual arousal is not expressed through appropriate sexual or social actions.

Pictorial representations of sexual activity lend themselves to the same approach. Unlike films and more like written materials, their use is essentially private. Nonetheless, patterns of use remain congruent with other patterns of social life and process; they represent anything but the triggering mechanisms through which the social contract is nullified and raging, unsocial lust (whatever that might be) is unleashed. The major users of pictorial erotica are adolescent males. If these materials have any use, it is as an aid to masturbation. There is no evidence, however, that the availability of dirty pictures increases masturbatory rates among adolescents. This is a period in life when masturbatory rates are already extremely high, particularly for middle class adolescents. Indeed, in the absence of hard-core pornography, the boys create their own stimulation from mail-order catalogues, magazine ads, and so on. In middle class circles, many young men and the majority of females may grow up without ever having seen hard-core pornography.

If exposure to this kind of pornography, while facilitating masturbation, does not substantially affect masturbatory rates, it is still possible that such materials may shape the content of the masturbatory fantasy in ways that create or reinforce commitments to sexual practices that are harmful to the individual or to others. In this area little is known. It may be observed that most pornographic materials share with the masturbatory fantasy a sense of omnipotence, but the acts represented are rarely homosexual, nor are they sadistic beyond the general levels of violence common in contemporary kitsch. Once again, one suspects a reinforcing or facilitating function rather than one of initiation or creation.

The pornographic book, in contrast to photographs and films, represents a very different social situation. Few books are read aloud in our society, and it is very unlikely that this would occur with a book of descriptions of overt sexual activity. In fact, prosecutors take advantage of this by reading allegedly obscene books aloud in court with the aim of embarrassing the jury into a guilty verdict. The privately consumed erotic book merely provides fantasy content or reinforcement of fantasy that is already established. Few books lead to overt action of any kind, and the erotic book is unlikely to be an exception.

The most difficult problem in considering pornography is the fringeland found on newsstands: the pulp books, national tabloids, men's magazines, and pinup collections which line the racks in drugstores, bus stations, and rail and air terminals. The girlie magazines are often under attack for nude pictures. The current magic line of censorship is pubic hair, though recently it was the bare breast or exposed nipple. Not so very long ago, navels were ruthlessly airbrushed away and Jane Russell's cleavage was an issue in gaining the censor's approval of the movie "Outlaw." The Gay Nineties were made gayer with pinups of strapping beauties clad in tights revealing only the bare flesh of face and hands.

In our era the pulp book freely describes most sexual activity with some degree of accuracy, although less explicitly and more metaphorically than hard-core pornographic pulp books. Such books are clearly published for their capacity to elicit sexual arousal, and they are purchased by an audience that knows what it is buying.

To view these examples of fringe pornography exclusively in terms of a sexual function might well be misleading. Since we tend to overestimate the significance of sexual activity, we see the trends of representation in these works as indicators of sexual behavior in the community. An increase in works about homosexual love is taken as an indication of an incipient homosexual revolution or even as the cause of a homosexual revolution. If we find more books about adultery, sadomasochism, or fast-living teenagers, we believe that there must be more adulterers, sado-masochists, and fast-living teenagers in our midst. With a dubious logic reminiscent of primitive magic, many believe that if the number of such representations increases, so will the frequency of such acts, and conversely that the way to cut down on this antisocial behavior is to suppress the pornographic representations.

In the fringeland there is a greater attempt to place sexual activity in the context of a social script, with a greater concern for nonsexual social relations and social roles, and a more direct treatment of appropriate social norms. Some part of this, particularly its common trait of compulsive moralizing, is an attempt to establish a spurious —but defensible under the Roth decision—"redeeming context." This may also represent the producer's awareness that more than simple lust is involved, that the reader may bring to the work a complex of motives, many of which are nonsexual.

For example, the psychiatrist Lionel Ovesey links some of the fantasies of his homosexual patients not to their sexual commitments, but to their problems of managing other personal relations, particularly in their jobs. The management of dominance or aggression in nonsexual spheres of life or the management of ideologies and moralities of social mobility may be the organizing mechanisms of such fantasies while sexuality provides an accessible and powerful imagery through which these other social tensions may be vicariously acted upon. Possibly it is overly simplistic to view this marginal pornography merely as something exclusively sexual.

These items at the fringeland are of most concern in the formulation of community standards. The girlie magazine and the pulp book are visible and priced within the range of the mass market. The hardcover book available at a high price in a bookstore may well cause no comment until it goes on the drugstore racks in paperback. Because such items are sold at breaks in transportation or in locations that tap neighborhood markets, they are the most visible portion of the problem and are the source of the discontent among those who are committed to censorship.

The dilemma, then, becomes the formulation of community standards, and this has been the dilemma of the courts themselves. One interesting attempt to strengthen enforcement of conservative standards is the interpretation of federal law to allow prosecution of a seller in the jurisdiction in which materials are received rather than in the ones from which they are mailed. Thus in the rather liberal jurisdiction of New York, where the sale of obscene materials must be compared in the mind of the judge with all the other kinds of crimes that come before him, the seller may well be seen as a small-timer, his crime a misdemeanor. However, in a rural jurisdiction where religious standards are more conservative and a pornography offense is viewed more seriously—especially when compared with the strayed cows and traffic violations that make up the most of the court docket—the seller is a heinous criminal.

The Supreme Court may wish to establish a national standard, allowing some jurisdictions to be more liberal but none to be more conservative. Thus the Supreme Court may build a floor under the right of materials to be protected under the First Amendment, at the same time constraining, through the use of the Ginzburg decision, the importation of materials through wide mailing campaigns into conservative communities. In its more recent decision, the court indicated—somewhat Delphically—that its concern in the future would be with three areas, none of them directly concerned with the content of any works charged as pornographic. These were sales of smut to minors, obtrusive presentation, and "pandering" *a la* Ginzburg. The court's decisions, however, may well be too conservative in a period when a national society is being created through penetration by the mass media of larger and larger elements of the society. Indeed, it is likely that most legal revolutions have been imposed from above and that communities will fall back to the set floor, if allowed to do so.

Pornography is as elusive as mercury. That of the past often no longer fills the bill. The use and users of contemporary pornography vary. Indeed, it might be said that sex itself would not change if there were no more pornography. Pornography is only a minor symptom of sexuality and of very little prominence in people's minds most of the time. Even among those who might think about it most, it results either in masturbation or in the "collector" instinct.

What is most important about pornography is not that it is particularly relevant to sexuality, but that it elicits very special treatment when it confronts the law. In this confrontation the agencies of criminal justice, and especially the courts, behave in a very curious manner that is quite dangerous for the freedom of ideas as they might be expressed in other zones of activity such as politics, religion, or the family. Our best protection in this regard has been the very contradictory character of the courts which carefully excludes the consideration of sexual ideas from the general test of the expression of ideas: Do they give rise to a clear and present danger? Our problem is not that pornography represents such a danger—it is far too minor a phenomenon for that—but that the kind of thinking prevalent in dealing with pornography will come to be prevalent in controlling the advocacy of other ideas as well.

July / August 1967

FURTHER READING SUGGESTED BY THE AUTHORS:

The Other Victorians by Steven Marcus (New York City: Basic Books, Inc., 1964). The social, literary, and psychoanalytic study of Victorian pornography by a distinguished critic.

Hustlers, Beats, and Others by Ned Polsky (Chicago: Aldine Publishing Co., 1967). The most explicit treatment of pornography from a sociological perspective.

Language and Silence: Essays in Language, Literature and the Inhuman edited by G. Steiner (New York City: Atheneum Publishers, 1967). See "Night Words" by George Steiner, a consideration of the impact of pornography on public language and private fantasy.

Eros Denied, Part III by Wayland Young (New York City: Grove Press, Inc., 1964). A defense of the role of pornography in society.

SELECTED BIBLIOGRAPHY

Abernathy, M. Glenn, *Civil Liberties and the Constitution.* New York: Dodd, Mead, 1968.

Abraham, Henry J., *The Judicial Process: An Introductory Analysis of the Courts of the United States, England, and France.* (2nd ed.) New York: Oxford University Press, 1968.

Alex, Nicholas, *Black in Blue.* New York: Appleton-Century-Crofts, 1969.

Alexander, Franz G., and Selesnick, Sheldon T., *The History of Psychiatry.* New York: Harper and Row, 1966.

Allen, Francis A., *The Borderland of Criminal Justice: Essays on Law and Criminology.* Chicago: University of Chicago Press, 1964.

Allen, Richard C., Ferster, Elyce Zenoff, and Rubin, Jesse G. (eds.) *Readings in Law and Psychiatry.* Baltimore, Md.: Johns Hopkins Press, 1968.

Arendt, Hannah, *Eichmann in Jerusalem.* New York: The Viking Press, 1963.

Arens, Richard and Lasswell, Harold D., *In Defense of Public Order: The Emerging Field of Sanction Law.* New York: Columbia University Press, 1961.

Asbury, Herbert, *The Gangs of New York.* New York: Alfred A. Knopf, 1928.

Aubert, Vilhelm, *The Hidden Society.* Totowa, N. J.: The Bedminster Press, 1965.

Bacon, Selden D., *The Early Development of American Municipal Police: A Study of the Evolution of Formal Control in a Changing Society.* Unpublished Ph.D. dissertation. Yale University, New Haven, 1939.

Baker, Joseph, *The Law of Political Uniforms, Public Meetings and Private Armies.* London: H. J. Just, 1937.

Banton, Michael, *The Policeman in the Community.* New York: Basic Books Inc., 1965.

Barth, Alan, *Law Enforcement versus the Law.* New York: Collier Books, 1963.

Bayley, David H., and Mendelsohn, Harold, *Minorities and the Police.* New York: The Free Press, 1969.

Becker, Harold K., *Law Enforcement: A Selected Bibliography.* Metuchen, N. J.: Scarecrow Press Inc., 1968.

Becker, Howard S., *Outsiders: Studies in the Sociology of Deviance.* New York: The Free Press, 1963.

Bedford, Sybille, *The Trial of Dr. Adams.* New York: Simon and Schuster, 1958.

Bell, Daniel, *The End of Ideology.* New York: Macmillan, 1958.

Belli, Melvin, *Dallas Justice.* New York: David McKay Co., 1964.

Benjamin, Harry and Masters, R.E.L., *Prostitution and Morality.* New York: Julian Press, 1964.

Berger, Morroe, *Equality by Statute: The Revolution in Civil Rights.* (revised ed.) Garden City, N. Y.: Doubleday, 1967.

Berman, Harold J., *Justice in the U.S.S.R.* (revised ed.) New York: Vintage Books, 1963.

Bedau, Hugo A. (ed.), *The Death Penalty in America.* Chicago: Aldine Publishing Co., 1964.

Bird, Otto A., *The Idea of Justice.* New York: Frederick A. Praeger, 1967.

Black, Algernon D., *The People and the Police.* New York: McGraw-Hill, 1968.

Blau, Peter M., *The Dynamics of Bureaucracy.* Chicago: University of Chicago Press, 1966.

Blaustein, Albert P., *The American Lawyer.* Chicago: University of Chicago Press, 1954.

Blum, Richard H. (ed.). *Police Selection.* Springfield, Ill.: Charles C. Thomas, 1964.

Blumberg, Abraham S., *The Criminal Court: An Organizational Analysis.* Unpublished Ph.D. dissertation, New School for Social Research, New York, 1965.

———— *Criminal Justice.* Chicago: Quadrangle Books, 1967.

Bordua, David J., *The Police: Six Sociological Essays.* New York: John Wiley and Sons, 1967.

Bornecque-Winancy, E., *Histoire de la Police.* Paris: Les Editiones Int., 1950.

Boskin, Joseph, *Urban Racial Violence in the Twentieth Century.* Beverly Hills, Calif.: Glencoe Press, 1969.

Bramsted, Ernest J., *Dictatorship and Political Police.* London: Routledge and Kegan Paul, 1945.

Brant, Irving, *The Bill of Rights.* New York: New American Library, 1967.

Bromberg, Walter, *Crime and the Mind.* New York: Funk & Wagnalls, 1968.

Brown, Wenzell, *Women Who Died in the Chair.* New York: Collier Books, 1963.

Buisson, Henry, *La Police, Son Histoire.* Paris: Nouvelles Editiones Latines, 1958.

Cairns, Huntington, *Law and the Social Sciences.* New York: Harcourt, Brace and World, 1935.

Camus, Albert, *The Stranger.* New York: Vintage Books, 1964.

Caplovitz, David, *The Poor Pay More.* New York: The Free Press, 1963.

Caplow, Theodore, *Principles of Organization.* New York: Harcourt, Brace and World, 1964.

Cardoza, Benjamin, *The Nature of the Judicial Process.* New Haven, Conn.: Yale University Press, 1931.

Carlin, Jerome E., Howard, Jan and Messinger, Sheldon L., *Civil Justice and the Poor: Issues for Sociological Research.* New York: Russell Sage Foundation, 1967.

———— *Lawyer's Ethics,* New York: Russell Sage Foundation, 1966.

———— *Lawyers on Their Own.* New Brunswick, N. J.: Rutgers University Press, 1962.

Carmichael, Stokely and Hamilton, Charles, *Black Power: The Politics of Liberation in America.* New York: Vintage Books, 1967.

Chambliss, William, *Crime and the Legal Process.* New York: McGraw-Hill, 1969.

Chapman, Samuel G., *The Police Heritage in England and America.* East Lansing, Mich.: Michigan State University Press, 1962.

Chevigny, Paul, *Police Power: Police Abuses in New York City.* New York: Pantheon, 1969.

Cicourel, Aaron V., *The Social Organization of Juvenile Justice.* New York: John Wiley and Sons, 1968.

Cipes, Robert M., *The Crime War.* New York: New American Library, 1968.

Clark, Kenneth B., *Dark Ghetto.* New York: Harper and Row, 1965.

Cleaver, Eldridge, *Soul on Ice.* New York: Delta Books, 1968.

Clegg, Reed K., *Probation and Parole.* Springfield, Ill.: Charles C. Thomas, 1964.

Cloward, Richard A., and Ohlin, Lloyd E., *Delinquency and Opportunity.* New York: The Free Press, 1960.

Conot, Robert, *Rivers of Blood, Years of Darkness.* New York: Bantam Books, 1967.

Cook, Fred J., *The Corrupted Land.* New York: Macmillan, 1966.

———— *The F.B.I. Nobody Knows.* New York: Macmillan, 1964.

———— *The Secret Rulers.* New York: Duell, Sloan and Pearce, 1966.

Cramer, James, *The World's Police.* London: Cassell and Co., Ltd., 1964.

Cray, Ed, *The Big Blue Line.* New York: Coward-McCann, Inc., 1967.

Cressey, Donald R. and Ward, David A., *Delinquency, Crime and Social Process.* New York: Harper and Row, 1969.

———— *Theft of the Nation.* New York: Harper and Row, 1969.

Curran, William J., *Law and Medicine.* Boston: Little, Brown and Co., 1960.

Dahl, Robert A., *Pluralist Democracy in the United States: Conflict and Consent.* Chicago: Rand McNally, 1967.

Darrow, Clarence, *The Story of My Life.* New York: Scribner's, 1934.

Dash, Samuel, Knowlton, Robert and Schwartz, Richard, *The Eavesdroppers.* New Brunswick, N. J.: Rutgers University Press, 1959.

Deutsch, Albert, *The Trouble with Cops.* New York: Crown Publishers Inc., 1955.

Dickens, Charles, *Bleak House*. London: J. M. Dent and Sons, Ltd., 1907.

Donnelly, Richard, Goldstein, J and Schwartz, Richard D., *Criminal Law*. New York: The Free Press, 1962.

Dressler, David, *Practice and Theory of Probation and Parole*. New York: Columbia University Press, 1959.

Durkheim, Emile, *The Division of Labor In Society*. New York: Macmillan, 1933.

———— *The Rules of Sociological Method*. New York: The Free Press, 1964.

Eidelberg, Paul, *The Philosophy of the American Constitution: A Reinterpretation of the Intentions of the Founding Fathers*. New York: The Free Press, 1968.

Eisner, Victor, *The Delinquency Label*. New York: Random House, 1968.

Emerson, Robert M., *Judging Delinquents: Context and Process in Juvenile Court*. Chicago: Aldine Publishing Co., 1969.

Erikson, Kai T., *Wayward Puritans*. New York: John Wiley and Sons, 1966.

Etzioni, Amitai, *A Comparative Analysis of Complex Organizations*. New York: The Free Press, 1964.

Evan, William M., ed., *Law and Sociology: Exploratory Essays*. New York: The Free Press, 1962.

Eysenck, H. J., *Crime and Personality*. Boston: Houghton Mifflin Co., 1964.

Falk, Richard A., *Legal Order in a Violent World*. Princeton, N. J.: Princeton University Press, 1968.

Faralicq, Rene, *The French Police from Within*. London: Cassell and Co., 1933.

Feifer, George, *Justice in Moscow*. New York: Simon and Schuster, 1964.

Ferri, Enrico, *Criminal Sociology*. New York: Appleton, 1896.

Fontana, Vincent J., *The Maltreated Child*. Springfield, Ill.: Charles C. Thomas, 1964.

Ford, Gerald R.; and Stiles, John R., *Portrait of the Assassin*. New York: Simon and Schuster, 1965.

Fosdick, Raymond, *European Police Systems*. New York: Century Company, 1915.

Frank, Jerome, *Courts on Trial*. Princeton, N. J.: Princeton University Press, 1949.

———— *Law and the Modern Mind*. New York: Tudor Publishing Co., 1935.

Frankfurter, Felix, *The Case of Sacco and Vanzetti*. Boston: Little, Brown and Co., 1927.

Freund, Paul A., *On Law and Justice*. Cambridge, Mass.: Harvard University Press, 1968.

Friendly, Alfred and Goldfarb, Ronald, *Crime and Publicity*. New York: Twentieth Century Fund, 1967.

Fuller, Lon L., *The Morality of Law*. New Haven, Conn.: Yale University Press, 1964.

Gagnon, John H. and Simon, William, *Sexual Deviance*. New York: Harper and Row, 1967.

Gebhard, Paul H., Gagnon, John H., Pomeroy, Wardell B., and Christenson, Cornelia V., *Sex Offenders: An Analysis of Types*. New York: Harper and Row, 1965.

Gellhorn, Walter, *Ombudsmen and Others: Citizen Protectors in Nine Countries*. Cambridge, Mass.: Harvard University Press, 1966.

Germann, A. C., Day, Frank D. and Gallati, Robert R. J., *Introduction to Law Enforcement*. Springfield, Ill.: Charles C. Thomas, 1962.

Giallombardo, Rose, *Society of Women*. New York: John Wiley and Sons, 1966.

Goffman, Erving, *Asylums*. Garden City, N. Y.: Doubleday-Anchor Books, 1961.

Goldfarb, Ronald, *Ransom*. New York: Harper and Row, 1965.

Goldman, Nathan, *The Differential Selection of Juvenile Offenders for Court Appearance*. New York: National Council on Crime and Delinquency, 1963.

Goldstein, Abraham S., *The Insanity Defense*. New Haven, Conn.: Yale University Press, 1967.

Graham, Hugh D. and Gurr, Ted R., *Violence in America*. New York: Signet Books, 1969.

Green, Edward, *Judicial Attitudes in Sentencing*. New York: St. Martin's Press, 1961.

Guttmacher, Manfred S. and Weihofen, Henry, *Psychiatry and the Law*. New York: W. W. Norton and Co., 1952.

Hall, Jerome, *Theft, Law and Society* (2nd ed.). Indianapolis: Bobbs-Merrill Co., 1952.

Halleck, Seymour L., *Psychiatry and the Dilemmas of Crime*. New York: Harper and Row, 1967.

Hart, H. L. A., *The Concept of Law*. London: Oxford University Press, 1961.

————— *Law, Liberty and Morality*. Stanford, Calif.: Stanford University Press, 1963.

————— *Punishment and Responsibility: Essays in the Philosophy of Law*. New York: Oxford University Press, 1967.

Hart, J. M., *The British Police*. London: Allen and Unwin, 1951.

Heller, Joseph. *Catch-22*. New York: Dell Publishing Co., 1961.

Henry, Andrew F. and Short, James F., Jr., *Suicide and Homicide*. New York: The Free Press, 1964.

Hersey, John, *The Algiers Motel Incident*. New York: Alfred A. Knopf, 1968.

Hewitt, William H., *A Bibliography of Police Administration, Public Safety and Criminology*. Springfield, Ill.: Charles C. Thomas, 1967.

182 / BIBLIOGRAPHY

——— British Police Administration. Springfield, Ill., Charles C. Thomas, 1965.

Hilberg, Raul, The Destruction of the European Jews. Chicago: Quadrangle Books, Inc., 1961.

Hobbes, Thomas, Leviathan. New York: E. P. Dutton and Co., Inc., 1950.

Hoebel, E. Adamson and Llewellyn, Karl N., The Cheyenne Way. Norman, Okla.: University of Oklahoma Press, 1941:

——— The Law of Primitive Man. Cambridge, Mass.: Harvard University Press, 1954.

Hofstadter, Richard, The Paranoid Style in American Politics. New York: Alfred A. Knopf, 1965.

Holmes, Oliver Wendell, The Common Law. (Edited by Mark DeWolfe Howe.) Cambridge, Mass.: Belknap Press of Harvard University Press, 1963.

Honnold, John, The Life of the Law. New York: The Free Press, 1964.

Hurst, James W., The Growth of American Law: The Law Makers. Boston: Little, Brown and Co., 1950.

Inbau, Fred E. and Reid, John E., Criminal Interrogation and Confessions. Baltimore, Md.: Williams and Wilkins, 1962.

——— and Sowle, Calude R., Criminal Justice: Cases and Comments. Brooklyn, N. Y.: The Foundation Press, 1964.

Jacobs, Paul, Prelude to Riot. New York: Random House, 1968.

Janowitz, Morris, Social Control of Esclated Riots. Chicago: University of Chicago Center for Policy Study, 1968.

Jaspan, Norman with Black, Hillel, The Thief in the White Collar. New York: J.B. Lippincott Co., 1960.

Jeffrey, Sir Charles, The Colonial Police. London: M. Parrish, 1952.

Johnson, Richard M., The Dynamics of Compliance: Supreme Court Decision-Making From a New Perspective. Evanston, Ill.: Northwestern University Press, 1968.

Jones, Alfred W., Life, Liberty, and Property. New York: Octagon Books, 1964.

Jones, Harry W., ed., The Courts, the Public, and the Law Explosion. Englewood Cliffs, N.J.: Prentice-Hall, 1965.

——— Law and the Social Role of Science. New York: Rockefeller University Press, 1967.

Jordan, Winthrop D., White Over Black. Baltimore, Md.: Pelican Books, 1969.

Josephson, Matthew, The Robber Barons. New York: Harcourt, Brace and World, 1962.

Kafka, Franz, The Trial. New York: Vintage Books, 1969.

Kalven, Harry, Jr. and Zeisel, Hans, The American Jury. Boston: Little, Brown and Co., 1966.

Kamisar, Yale, Inbau, Fred and Arnold, Thurman, Criminal Justice in Our Time. Charlottesville, Va.: The University Press of Virginia, 1965.

Karlen, Delmar, *Anglo-American Criminal Justice.* New York: Oxford University Press, 1967.

———— *The Supreme Court and Political Freedom.* New York: The Free Press, 1968.

Karpman, Benjamin, *The Sexual Offender and His Offenses.* New York: Julian Press, 1954.

Kefauver, Estes, *Crime in America.* New York: Doubleday, 1951.

Keller, Suzanne, *Beyond the Ruling Class.* New York: Random House, 1963.

Kennedy, Robert F., *The Pursuit of Justice.* New York: Harper and Row, 1964.

Kenny, John P. and Pursuit, Dan G., *Police Work with Juveniles.* (3rd ed.). Springfield, Ill.: Charles C. Thomas, 1965.

Kephart, William M., *Racial Factors and Urban Law Enforcement.* Philadelphia: University of Pennsylvania, 1957.

Kirchheimer, Otto, *Political Justice.* Princeton, N. J.: Princeton University Press, 1961

Krislov, Samuel, *The Supreme Court and Political Freedom.* New York: The Free Press, 1968.

Kronhausen, Eberhard and Kronhausen, Phyllis, *Pornography and the Law.* New York: Ballantine Books, 1959.

LaFave, Wayne R., *Arrest: The Decision to Take a Suspect into Custody.* Boston: Little, Brown and Co., 1965.

Lane, Roger, *Policing the City: Boston 1822-1882.* Cambridge, Mass.: Harvard University Press, 1967.

Leopold, Nathan F., *Life Plus 99 Years.* New York: Doubleday, 1958.

Levi, Primo, *Survival in Auschwitz.* New York: Collier Books, 1961.

Liebow, Elliot, *Tally's Corner.* Boston: Little, Brown and Co., 1967.

Lindesmith, Alfred R., *The Addict and the Law.* Bloomington, Ind.: Indiana University Press, 1965.

Lipset, Seymour M., *Political Man.* Garden City, N. Y.: Doubleday and Co., 1960.

Lofton, John, *Justice and the Press.* Boston: Beacon Press, 1966.

Lorenz, Konrad, Marjorie Wilson, tr. *On Aggression.* New York: Harcourt, Brace and World, 1966.

Lowenthal, Max, *The Federal Bureau of Investigation.* New York: Sloane Associates, 1950.

Maine, Sir Henry J., *Ancient Law.* London and Toronto: J.M. Dent and Sons; New York: E.P. Dutton and Co., 1931.

Mannheim, Hermann, *Comparative Criminology.* Boston: Houghton Mifflin Co., 1965.

———— (ed.) *Pioneers in Criminology.* Chicago: Quadrangle Books, 1960.

Marshall, Geoffrey, *Police and Government.* London: Mathuen and Co., 1965.

Marshall, James, *Intention in Law and Society*. New York: Funk and Wagnalls, 1968.

———— *Law and Psychology in Conflict*. Garden City, N. Y.: Doubleday-Anchor, 1969.

Marx, Gary T., *Protest and Prejudice*. New York: Harper and Row, 1969.

Mayers, Lewis, *The American Legal System*. New York: Harper and Row, 1964.

McCague, James, *The Second Rebellion: The Story of the New York City Draft Riots of 1863*. New York: Dial Press, 1968.

Medalie, Richard J., *From Escobedo to Miranda*. Washington, D. C.: Lerner Law Book Co., 1966.

Menninger, Karl, *The Crime of Punishment*. New York: The Viking Press, 1968.

———— *The Vital Balance*. New York: The Viking Press, 1964.

Michael, Jerome and Adler, Mortimer, *Crime, Law and Social Science*. New York: Harcourt, Brace and Co., 1933.

Mitford, Jessica, The Trial of Dr. Spock, New York: Alfred A. Knopf, 1969.

Mollenhoff, Clark, *Tentacles of Power: The Story of Jimmy Hoffa*. Cleveland: The World Publishing Co., 1965.

Murphy, Walter F. and Pritchett, C. Herman, *Courts, Judges and Politics*. New York: Random House, 1961.

Myers, Gustavus, *History of the Great American Fortunes*. New York: Modern Library, 1936.

Neumann, Franz, *Behemoth*. London: V. Gollancz, 1942.

Newman, Donald J., *Conviction: The Determination of Guilt or Innocence Without Trial*. Boston: Little, Brown and Co., 1966.

Niederhoffer, Arthur, *Behind the Shield*. Garden City, N. Y.: Doubleday and Co., 1967.

———— *A Study of Police Cynicism*. Unpublished doctoral dissertation. New York University, N.Y., 1964.

Norman, Charles, *The Genteel Murderer*. New York: Collier Books, 1962.

Nye, F. Ivan, *Family Relationships and Delinquent Behavior*. New York: John Wiley and Sons, 1958.

Oaks, Dallin H. and Lehman, Warren, *A Criminal Justice System and the Indigent: A Study of Chicago and Cook County*. Chicago: University of Chicago Press, 1968.

O'Gorman, Hubert J., *Lawyers and Matrimonial Cases*. New York: The Free Press, 1963.

Packer, Herbert L., *The Limits of the Criminal Sanction*. Stanford, Calif.: Stanford University Press, 1968.

Pearlstein, Stanley, *Psychiatry, the Law and Mental Health*. Dobbs Ferry, N.Y.: Oceana Publications, 1967.

Peltason, Jack W., *Federal Courts in the Political Process*. Garden City, N. Y. Doubleday, 1955.

Platt, Anthony, *The Child Savers: The Invention of Delinquency.* Chicago: University of Chicago Press, 1969.

Ploscowe, Morris, *Sex and the Law.* New York: Ace Books, 1962.

Polier, Justine W., *The Rule of Law and the Role of Psychiatry.* Baltimore, Md.: Johns Hopkins Press, 1968.

Porterfield, Austin L., *Youth in Trouble.* Fort Worth: Leo Potishman Foundation, 1946.

Pound, Roscoe, *Social Control Through Law.* New Haven, Conn.: Yale University Press, 1942.

President's Commission on Law Enforcement and Administration of Justice. Task Force Reports: The Police; the Courts; Corrections; Juvenile Delinquency and Youth Crime; Organized Crime; Science and Technology; Assessment of Crime; Narcotics and Drugs; Drunkenness. Washington, D.C.: U.S. Government Printing Office, 1967.

Pritchett, C. Herman, *The American Constitution* (2nd ed.) New York: McGraw-Hill, 1968.

Puttkammer, Ernest W., *Administration of Criminal Law.* Chicago: University of Chicago Press, 1963.

Quinney, Richard, ed., *Crime and Justice in Society.* Boston: Little, Brown and Co., 1969.

Raab, Selwyn, *Justice in the Back Room.* Cleveland: The World Publishing Co., 1967.

Radzinowicz, Leon, *A History of English Criminal Law and Its Administration from 1750* Vols. 1-4. New York: Barnes and Noble, 1968.

Ray, Isaac, *A Treatise on the Medical Jurisprudence of Insanity.* Winfred Overholser, ed., Cambridge, Mass.: Harvard University Press, 1962.

Reith, Charles, *The Blind Eye of History.* London: Faber and Faber, 1952.

——————— *A New Study of Police History.* London: Oliver and Boyd, 1956.

Rheinstein, Max, ed., *Max Weber on Law in Economy and Society.* trans. by E. Shils and M. Rheinstein. Cambridge, Mass.: Harvard University Press, 1954.

Richardson, James, *A History of Police Protection in New York City, 1800-1870.* Unpublished Ph.D. dissertation. New York City: New York University, 1967.

Rolph, C.H., ed., *The Police and the Public.* London: Heinemann, 1962.

Rose, Arnold M., *Libel and Academic Freedom: A Lawsuit Against Political Extremists.* Minneapolis: University of Minnesota Press, 1968.

Rosenberg, Charles E., *The Trial of Assassin Guiteau: Psychiatry and Law in the Guilded Age.* Chicago: University of Chicago Press, 1968.

Royal Commission on the Police, 1962, *Final Report,* Cmnd. 1728. London: Her Majesty's Stationery Office, 1962.

Scheff, Thomas J., (ed.), *Mental Illness and Social Processes*. New York: Harper and Row, 1967.

Schneir, Walter and Schneir, Marian, *Invitation to an Inquest*. New York: Doubleday, 1965.

Schubert, Glendon, ed., *Judicial Behavior*. Chicago: Rand McNally, 1964.

————— *Judicial Decision-Making*. New York: The Free Press, 1963.

Schur, Edwin M., *Crimes Without Victims*. Englewood Cliffs, N. J. Prentice-Hall, 1965.

————— *Drug Addiction in America and England*. Bloomington, Ind.: Indiana University Press, 1962.

————— *Law and Society: A Sociological View*. New York: Random House, 1968.

Scigliano, Robert G., *The Courts: A Reader in the Judicial Process*. Boston: Little, Brown and Co., 1962.

Seligman, Ben B., *Permanent Poverty: An American Syndrome*. Chicago: Quadrangle Books, 1968.

Shaw, George Bernard, *The Crime of Imprisonment*. New York: The Citadel Press, 1961.

Shoolbred, Claude F., *The Administration of Criminal Justice in England and Wales*. New York: Pergamon Press, 1966.

Simon, Rita James, *The Jury and the Plea of Insanity*. Boston: Little, Brown and Co., 1966.

————— (ed.), *The Sociology of law: Interdisciplinary Readings*. San Francisco, Calif.: Chandler, 1968.

Skolnick, Jerome H., *Justice Without Trial: Law Enforcement in Democratic Society*. New York: John Wiley and Sons, 1966.

————— *The Politics of Protest*. New York: Ballantine Books, 1969.

Smigel, Erwin O., *The Wall Street Lawyer*. New York: The Free Press,

Smith, Alexander B. and Neiderhoffer, Arthur, *Police-Community Relations Programs: A Study in Depth*. Washington, D.C.: U.S. Government Printing Office, 1969.

Smith, Bruce, *The New York Police Survey*. New York: Institute of Public Administration, 1952.

————— *Police Systems in the United States* (2nd rev. ed.) New York: Harper and Row, 1960.

Smith, Ralph L., *The Tarnished Badge*. New York: Thomas Y. Crowell Co., 1965.

Solmes, Alwyn, *The English Policeman, 1871-1935*. London: George Allen and Unwin, 1935.

Sowle, Claude R. (ed.), *Police Power and Individual Freedom*. Chicago: Aldine Publishing Co., 1962.

Starkey, Marion L., *The Devil in Massachusetts*. New York: Alfred A. Knopf, 1950.

Steffens, Lincoln, *Autobiography*. New York: Harcourt, Brace and World, 1936.

——— *The Shame of the Cities*. New York: McClure Phillips and Co., 1904.

Sutherland, Arthur E., *Constitutionalism in America*. Boston: Blaisdell Publishing Co., 1965.

Sutherland, Edwin H., *White Collar Crime*. New York: Holt, Rinehart and Winston, 1949.

Sykes, Gresham, *Society of Captives*. Princeton, N. J.: Princeton University Press, 1958.

——— and Drobek, Thomas E., *Law and the Lawless*. New York: Random House,, 1969.

Szasz, Thomas, *Law, Liberty and Psychiatry*. New York: Macmillan, 1963.

——— *Psychiatric Justice*. New York: Macmillan, 1965.

Tannenbaum, Frank, *Crime and the Community*. New York: Columbia University Press, 1938.

Thompson, Craig, *The Police State*. New York: E. P. Dutton and Co., 1950.

Thompson, Hunter S., *Hell's Angels*. New York: Random House, 1966.

Tiffany, Lawrence P., McIntyre, Donald M. Jr. and Rotenberg, David L., *Detection of Crime: Stopping and Questioning, Search and Seizure, Encouragement and Entrapment*. Boston: Little, Brown and Co., 1967.

Toch, Hans, *Violent Men: An Inquiry into the Psychology of Violence*. Chicago: Aldine Publishing Co., 1969.

Train, Arthur, *Courts, Criminals and the Camorra*. New York: C. Scribner's Sons, 1911.

Trebach, Arnold S., *The Rationing of Justice*. New Brunswick, N. J.: Rutgers University Press, 1964.

Turner, William, *The Police Establishment*. New York: G.P. Putnam and Sons, 1968.

Tyler, Gus, *Organized Crime in America*. Ann Arbor, Mich.: University of Michigan Press, 1962.

Virtue, Maxine, *Survey of Metropolitan Courts: Final Report*. Ann Arbor, Mich.: The University of Michigan Press, 1962.

Vollmer, August, *The Police and Modern Society*. Berkeley, Calif.: University of California Press, 1936.

Vollmer, Howard M. and Mills, Donald L., (eds.) *Professionalization*. Englewood Cliffs, N. J.: Prentice-Hall Inc., 1966.

Walker, Nigel, *Crime and Insanity in England: Vol. 1: the Historical Perspective*. Edinburgh, Scotland: Edinburgh University Press, 1968.

Wallace, Samuel E., *Skid Row As a Way of Life*. Ottowa: The Bedminster Press, 1965.

Weber, Max, *The Theory of Social and Economic Organization*. New York: The Free Press, 1964.

Wertham, Frederick, *A Sign for Cain.* New York: Macmillan, 1966.

Westley, William A., *The Police: A Sociological Study of Law, Custom and Mortality.* Unpublished dissertation, Ph.D. Department of Sociology, University of Chicago, Chicago, 1951.

Weyrauch, Walter O., *The Personality of Lawyers.* New Haven, Conn.: Yale University Press, 1964.

Whitaker, Ben, *The Police.* Middlesex, England: Penguin Books, 1964.

Whittmore, L. H., *Cop: A Closeup of Violence and Tragedy.* New York: Holt, Rinehart and Winston, 1969.

Wilkins, Leslie T., *Social Deviance.* Englewood Cliffs, N. J.: Prentice-Hall, Inc., 1965.

Whyte, William F., *Street Corner Society.* Chicago: University of Chicago Press, 1943.

Williams, Edward Bennett, *One Man's Freedom.* New York: Atheneum, 1962.

Wilson, James Q., *Varieties of Police Behavior.* Cambridge, Mass.: Harvard University Press, 1968.

Wilson, O. W., *Police Administration* (2nd ed.) New York: McGraw-Hill, 1963.

Wolfenden, Sir John and others, *Report of the Departmental Committee on Homosexual Offences and Prostitution.* London: Her Majesty's Stationery Office, 1956.

Wood, Arthur L., *Criminal Lawyer.* New Haven, Conn.: College and University Press, 1967.

Zeisel, Hans, Kalven, Harry Jr., and Buckholz, Bernard, *Delay in the Court.* Boston: Little, Brown and Co., 1959.